45 BINGE TRIGGER BUSTERS

How to Resist the Most Common Overeating Triggers Until They Lose Their Power Over You

Glenn Livingston Ph.D.

DISCLAIMER: For education only. You are responsible for determining your own nutritional, medical, and psychological needs. If you require assistance with this task you must consult with a licensed physician, nutritionist, psychologist, and/or other professional. No medical, psychological, and/or nutritional advice is offered through this book. Even though the author is a licensed psychologist, he does not offer psychological services, psychological advice and/or psychological counsel in his role as author of this book. In particular, if you have ever been diagnosed with an eating disorder you agree not to create your Food Plan and/or any Food Rules and/or to change your diet in any way without the input and approval of a psychiatrist, psychologist, and licensed dietician. Psy Tech Inc. and/or Never Ever Again, Inc. is only willing to license you the right to utilize this book in the event you agree with these terms. If you do not agree with these terms, please do not read the book, delete it from all electronic devices you own, and/or return it to your place of purchase for a full refund (where applicable).

CONTENTS

CHAPTER 1: INTRODUCTION TO THE NEVER BINGE AGAIN PHILOSOPHY

"It is no measure of health to be well adjusted to a profoundly sick society."

Jiddu Krishnamurti

In our culture it seems we have a tacit agreement to slowly kill ourselves with food.

We support each other to joke about it, deny it, and look the other way. Whenever any of us decides to forgo some of these indulgences, especially in public, we feel deprived, abnormal, and ostracized. And we have nary a thought for what we may be TRULY depriving ourselves of by continuing to indulge... health, well-being, energy, presence of mind, and longevity.

We've gotten to the point that virtually nobody in our culture can have a normal relationship with food unless they work very hard at it. "Normal" has been totally corrupted by Big Food, Big Advertising, and Big Addiction Treatment. For first time in millions of years of evolutionary history it's become "normal" to:

- ➢ Walk out of a McDonalds on one corner and see another one right across the street...
- ➢ Have an ocean of concentrated starch, sugar, oil, salt, etc. available to us for virtually no effort, at an extremely low price, and hardly any effort...
- ➢ Look the other way while your friends, family, coworkers, etc. slowly destroy themselves by piling garbage into their face-holes...

It's also "normal" for:

- ➢ 39.7% of men and 37.6% of women to get cancer in their lifetime *(the Mayo Clinic)* ...
- ➢ 26.5% of Americans to live with heart disease *(American Heart Association)* ...
- ➢ 100,000,000+ people in the USA alone to live with diabetes or pre-diabetes *(Center for Disease Control)*

Is this the normal you want? Is this the LIFE you want?

All these things may indeed be AVERAGE, but you can NOT convince me it's normal!

I suggest you decide right here and now to STOP striving to be "normal", and STOP comparing yourself to the average person around you. Instead, strive to be GREAT, because "normal" is horrendous. You can do MUCH better!

Some accuse me of grandiosity for taking this position, but I stand by my convictions, because by striving for greatness I accept and acknowledge I'm going to have to do things other people choose not to embrace. I'm going to have to work, for a brief period, to aggressively separate my constructive vs. destructive thinking, and lock my reptilian brain down tight so I can approximate what normality WOULD have looked like 10,000 years ago...before the profiteers of industry got their fangs in our necks. *(Did you ever stop to think that every time you look for love at the bottom of a bag, box, or container there's some fat cat in a white suit with a mustache laughing all the way to the bank!?)*

I OFFICIALLY OPT OUT OF NORMALITY AND YOU SHOULD TOO!

My first book "Never Binge Again" is a controversial-but-VERY-popular book on overcoming overeating and regaining full control over what you put in your mouth. At the time of this writing it has more than 2,000+ reviews on Amazon and has hovered at and/or near the #1 position in the weight loss category for almost three years. You can get the book for FREE in Kindle, Nook, or PDF format at www.NeverBingeAgain.com.

Never Binge Again promises you a NEW kind of control with food. Not the kind of grit-your-teeth and bear it control you may have experienced before while dieting, but lifelong, permanent control. On the diet of your choice! I know that's a big promise and I didn't make it lightly.

Never Binge Again *(my first book)* suggests you (1) create clear, bright lines that define healthy vs. unhealthy food and food behavior; (2) aggressively separate your constructive vs. destructive thinking about food, designating *constructive* thoughts as all those thoughts which support healthy behavior. And *destructive* thinking being all those thoughts which encourage you to cross the line; (3) act as if all your destructive thoughts originate from a fictitious mental entity we call "The Pig"; (4) decide You are the sum total of your constructive thinking and consciously separate yourself from The Pig. Then, when you have a Craving for something over the line, say to yourself "That's Pig Slop and I don't eat Pig Slop...I don't want that my Pig does! And I never let farm animals tell me what to do!"

You don't have to call it a "Pig" if that bothers you – Food Demon™, Food Monster™, etc. work just as well. You can call it whatever you want provided you think of it more as a bodily organ to be controlled vs. a cuddly pet or "inner wounded child" to be nurtured. You need to cultivate a sense of dominant control over it.

Never Binge Again also challenges several cultural myths which keep people in the modern world from successfully sticking to the diet of their choice and accomplishing their health and fitness goals.

The combination of the unusual mental trick above with the disempowerment of cultural mythology about food has given thousands and thousands of people an ability to control themselves (an ability they never had before). In many cases, it's given them their life back!

I never intended to publish the book. It was just a personal journal about a weird technique I used to beat my own Pig, stop obsessing about food, and drop 70 to 80 pounds after decades of slowly eating myself towards an early grave. I also dramatically increased my energy, radically reduced my blood lipids, and became symptom free from psoriasis, rosacea, eczema, and several other minor medical conditions. *(Note: That doesn't mean you will, but I did.)*

I edited my journal into the book now known as Never Binge Again in 2015 when I was a minor partner in a publishing company and the CEO asked me if I could write one. He wanted to market it and prove their worth so we could attract more valuable authors. So, I edited my eight years of journaling about the conversations I had with my Inner Pig into a book.

I then gave the book to him, and he devoured it. It started him on his own 86-pound weight loss journey! 600,000+ copies later it's been an amazing success. Did I mention you could *(and should)* read it for free? www.NeverBingeAgain.com

In case you just don't want to read another free book, here are the critical points in sum. At minimum it's important you understand how the Never Binge Again philosophy is radically different than conventionally accepted cultural norms. Only in this context will you be able to implement the Binge Trigger Busters effectively. *(If you've already read Never Binge Again you can skip this summary)*:

Myth Buster #1 - You Can Love Yourself Thin. *(You Can't!)*

Popular mythology holds that it's not what you're eating, it's what's eating *you* that keeps you overeating. Therefore, the thinking goes, you must learn love yourself and fill that hole in your heart if you want to stop. Unfortunately, this line of reasoning ignores two critical facts:

- ➢ The reptilian brain, that primitive neurological structure most responsible for addiction, doesn't know love – it only knows "eat, mate, or kill";
- ➢ Industry spends billions of dollars engineering food-like substances to override out best judgment. Their goal is to hit our bliss point without giving us enough nutrition to feel satisfied. They do it with hyperpalatable concentrations of starch, sugar, fat, oil, salt, and excitotoxins that hijack our brains and make us think we *need* all the bags, boxes, and containers they manufacture. In fact, we come to believe we need these bags, boxes, and contains much more so than what nature has to offer in order to survive. That's why people don't like fruit and vegetables so much anymore! Then Big Food spends a fortune on Big Advertising to make us believe it too. *(And if you think advertising doesn't affect you – think again! Advertising effects people more when they think it doesn't because their sales resistance is down.)*

The point is, these very strong forces are at work regardless of how much you love *(or don't love)* yourself, no matter what unresolved trauma you hold in your heart, and no matter how angry, lonely, sad, tired, happy, depressed, tired, and/or anxious you happen to get. It's perfectly fine if you want to nurture your inner wounded child back to health, just don't expect that endeavor to fix your eating or you'll be waiting *(and binging)* for a VERY long time!

Myth Buster #2 – Guidelines are Better Than Rules. *(They're Not!)*:

Guidelines require constant decision making about food, and decisions wear down your willpower. The research strongly suggests there are only so many good decisions we can make each day. So, if you say "I'm going to avoid chocolate 90% of the time and eat it 10%," you've put yourself in a very bad position. Now you'll have to make a chocolate decision every time you're in front of a bar at the checkout counter in Starbucks... and that takes a LOT of willpower!

In contrast, if you say "I'm only ever going to eat chocolate again on the last three days of the Calendar Month, and never more than 2 oz per Calendar Day" you've effectively accomplished the same 90/10 split *(3 days out of 30 is ten percent)*, except this time all your decisions are already made. No will power needed!

Ultimately what you've created with the latter strategy is a statement of character. It's not so much a rule as deciding to *become the kind of person* who only eats chocolate 3 days per calendar month. And in so doing you'll have discovered that *character trumps willpower.*

Guidelines are also WAY too easy for our Pigs to barrel through. For example, if you say "I avoid chocolate most of the time" and the Pig has a strong craving, how will you know whether TODAY is one of the days you must avoid it or not? When your Pig wants chocolate, all it will need to do is say: "You DO avoid chocolate most of the time, so let's have some TODAY!" What does "most" in "most of the time" mean? 90% of the time? 62% of the time? 51% of the time? Your guess is as good as mine. Or your Pig's.

Taken to its natural conclusion you'll see what "I avoid chocolate most of the time" really means is "I'll try to avoid chocolate until I don't feel like avoiding it anymore." Now, this might work for some skinny models, or people who don't really love chocolate... but for people with a serious chocolate problem it's NO help at all. In fact, it makes things worse by drawing attention to chocolate without providing a solid protection limit against it.

Food *guidelines* favor your Pig, but *rules* favor you!

On the other hand, "I'm only ever going to eat chocolate again on the last three days of the Calendar Month" is an unassailable food rule. Either it's the last three days of the month or it isn't. 10 neutral observers following you around all month would KNOW AND AGREE whether you kept to this 100% or not. The inclusion of the word "never" means "under any circumstances whatsoever" and excludes ALL possible exceptions your Pig may try to squeeze in. And the word "again" means "between now and the day the universe is no more" ...so the Pig can't say "Oh, well, you didn't really mean you were going to do that *forever*, did you?"

Unfortunately, over-eaters tend to favor *guidelines* because they believe it's impossible to vow anything forever. They fear excessive guilt and self-castigation when and if they make a mistake.

This is an erroneous understanding of the appropriate role for guilt in the psyche. Berating and scolding yourself for a mistake is the WRONG attitude when you make a mistake. If you screw up, you're supposed to take a hard look at what went wrong and figure out how to do better next time, NOT repeatedly smack yourself in the head with a spatula! In fact, the self-punishment which occurs for many over-eaters after a serious food mistake is really their Inner Pig trying to convince them they are too weak to hold to this rule... the Pig is trying to get them to do it *again! (For this reason, as I learned from Carol Munter, author of Overcoming Overeating, it's very difficult to keep binging if you refuse to yell at yourself.)*

Perfectionism is the wrong mindset *when looking back on your mistakes*, but the right *(and only)* mindset to take *when looking forward towards your goals*. For example, if you wanted to climb a mountain peak, you should visualize yourself victoriously enjoying the view from the top. Purge ALL doubt and distraction about the possibility of failure from your mind so you can concentrate your energy on accomplishing your goal. That's what winner's do!

If it really weren't possible to vow to do something forever, what justification could we possibly ever have for marriage? I've yet to hear the following vow at a wedding: *"I promise to love and be faithful...until an inevitable moment of weakness. I promise I'll do the best I can, but nobody's perfect and there sure are a lot of attractive people out there. I'm 80% sure I can be faithful forever, but anyone who promises you 100% is an unrealistic liar. A 'pretty good' promise is the best anyone can ever hope for, because you can't possibly know who you're going to sleep with next year, or in ten years. Just being honest. You want me to be honest, right?" – The Vow Your Pig Would Make at Its Wedding!*

A vow is a plan to remember... but your Pig wants you to plan to forget.

Cage the Pig and take control!

The benefit of declaring yourself 100% confident and 100% committed when you vow to follow a food RULE has another very strong benefit which most people don't realize...

It allows us to clearly separate the Pig's thoughts from our own. If you're willing to draw a crystal-clear line in the sand about a particular trigger food or behavior, then any thought, feeling, or impulse which suggests you might ever cross it again can be immediately dismissed as nothing more than your Pig Squealing for its junk. A 100% clear and confident commitment is a thinking tool which makes it possible to hear the Pig Squeal *(that seductive inner dialogue which suggests you're going to break your plan)*...so you can pause and choose wisely!

Myth Buster #3 – We Need to Be Frightened of Our Impulses. *(You Don't! Cultivate Confidence Instead!)*

Our culture also widely believes the impulse to overeat is irresistible to certain people in certain situations, and more importantly, that the only way to combat it is to form dependent relationships with accountability partners, rush to support groups, avoid tempting situations, get a sponsor, etc. Some go so far as suggesting overeating must be disease.

Never Binge Again doesn't buy into this mythology at all. Instead, we believe the problem is nothing more than a healthy appetite corrupted by industry for profit. Our best defense is to **confidently** define exactly where the line is between healthy vs. unhealthy eating for ourselves, then listen carefully for that destructive voice within us, and either ignore and/or disempower it while we otherwise thoroughly nourish our bodies.

We can become as confident in our ability to Never Binge Again as we are in our ability to never express our bladder in the middle of a business meeting without excusing ourselves to go to the bathroom. Most of us would NEVER just drop my pants and go right there and then because we've subjugated our bladder's very powerful biological urge to our human brain. We live comfortably with this biological need while insisting it be taken care of in a particular place, at a particular time, in a particular way. Food is no different.

We can also become 100% confident in our ability to do this *forever* because the only time you can stop overeating is NOW, and the future is an infinite string of NOWs. *(Thanks to Jack Trimpey of Rational Recovery for this insight).* You can't do anything about what you put in your mouth five years, five months, five days, or even five minutes ago...but you CAN use the present moment to be healthy. It is ALWAYS now and will ALWAYS BE now, so we CAN confidently declare our ability to ALWAYS eat healthy.

Cultivating a confident attitude helps you develop a success identity, and a success identity is what empowers you to Never Binge Again.

Therefore, Never Binge Again focuses on INTERNAL motivation. See, when it comes to weight loss, external motivation is a big problem. You could be listening to inspiring podcasts, reading energizing memes, and feel optimistic and bubbly 95% of the time...but during those 5% of times you feel down, when your outlook flips from optimism to pessimism, the Pig will binge and do major damage that erases the other 95% *(and more!)*

Never Binge Again arms you with an internal driving force to function even when you're feeling down and defeated. These are twelve sources of INTERNAL motivation:

- ➢ Separating yourself (your healthy food thoughts) from the Pig (unhealthy food thoughts) as per above
- ➢ Using internal dialog to gain control and lock the Pig in its Cage
- ➢ A list of logical, highly convincing disputations you can use

even when you are feeling down/depressed or anxious...

- Food rules that allow you to instantly identify the thoughts which precede a binge...
- A dramatic reduction of the internal chatter around food and diet due to your rules...
- A gradual change in your very character that ELIMINATES the need for will power...
- The ability to forgive yourself with respect and dignity for eating mistakes...
- Making a 100% commitment to your rules while having a mechanism to change them when necessary...
- The ability to "wake yourself up" at the moment of craving and harness the full power of your higher brain to cage the Pig before/ at the beginning of a binge...
- Creating your success satchel – a collection of previous successes that you can draw on in moments of weakness...
- Your Big Why...
- Your Biggest Why...
- Establishing a SELF-ACCOUNTABILITY routine that will make it 10 times more important for you to stick to your rules than submitting to your Inner Pig!

There's NO need to fear your impulse to overeat. As a matter of fact, you should welcome it...

Myth Buster #4 – Cravings are Signs of Trouble! *(They're Not! Every Craving is an Opportunity)*

Welcome Your Cravings Don't Fear Them! Many people who

overeat in our culture are terrified they'll get an "irresistible" craving. They walk around frightened of their own bodies, feeling like a slave to their own impulses. But Never Binge Again says that's NO way to live! Instead, we cultivate confidence, not fear, as per above. We believe WE are always in control despite what the Food Industry, the Advertising Industry, the Addiction Treatment Industry, and our Pigs would have us believe.

So, a craving is something to be WELCOMED, not tremble with fear in front of. It is only by experiencing your cravings that you get the opportunity to extinguish them. It is also only by experiencing your cravings that you get the opportunity to retrain your survival drive to point at what it genuinely needs... what nature intended. You can't kill a craving without experiencing it. You can't recapture your natural survival instinct without re-experiencing the corrupted craving.

Plus, behind every craving is almost always an AUTHENTIC NEED. Something you genuinely do need in order to feed your body or your mind, but profiteers in industry have seduced your survival drive into thinking it needs the wrong thing. You can't possibly "need" that bag of chips right now because there were no chips when we were evolving in the tropics – your body and your brain has made a biological error. Every bone in your body may believe you "need" that bag, box, or container, but FEELINGS AREN'T FACTS and you do NOT need Pig Slop to survive no matter how much it may FEEL like you do!

For example, I remember when I realized that if I ran to get some fruit, leafy greens, and/or kale-cucumber juice the moment I had a chocolate craving, the craving would go away. I didn't get the "food high" or level of unnatural pleasure which the chocolate bar would've provided me, but I DID kill the craving and felt a LOT more comfortable. And I fed my body the nutrition and energy boost it needed to get through the crucial moment. I could ignore the industrially induced desire.

After I did that a dozen times or so I started craving greens and fruit instead of chocolate bars... and it all happened a LOT faster than my Pig would have me believe it could. In about two months I very rarely experienced any desire for chocolate at all. After 18 months chocolate bars just started to look like big bags of chemicals to me. I look at them now and wonder how they ever had ANY power over me at all.

SEIZE EVERY CRAVING AS AN OPPORTUNITY TO EXTINGUISH THE CRAVING ITSELF, and to actively reprogram your body to crave what it needs instead. Your body WILL adjust!

Your Pig says this is impossible. "This can't possibly work!"

In fact, the Pig is often so loud at first that every bone in your body may FEEL as if this is crazy. That's why we have sayings like "Just hand over the chocolate and nobody gets hurt!"

But feelings aren't facts. You don't have to believe me, you only have to try it consistently for a while to see for yourself.

Myth Buster #5 – Hope and Pray for Relief. *(Don't Hope and Pray! Declare It and Make It Happen Instead!)*

In twelve step programs people are taught to seek conscious contact with God and pray that He remove their impulse to overeat. They are told they're powerless over their addictions and the best they can do is pray for God to remove their desire to act them out.

This is very odd when you think about it...

- ➢ First of all, every major religion suggests that we should behave well in order to please God, not ask God to MAKE us stop behaving badly.

➢ And secondly, why would God EVER remove the healthy desire to find calories and nutrition from us? Wasn't there a reason He put it there in the first place?

I'm admittedly not a religious person or even a scholar of the ancient books, so I'm not prepared to debate this in detail, but something seems very fishy on its surface, don't you think?

And even for non-religious people, why would you want to hope and pray for peace with food when you could take control and CREATE it for yourself.

DON'T HOPE AND PRAY FOR PEACE WITH FOOD!

Hoping, wishing, and praying for peace with food is just your Pig saying "Gee, I wish we could be one of the lucky ones - maybe if we hope and pray long enough we will be - but in the meantime you know what will make us feel better? Hmmmmmm??? Do ya? Go get us some Slop!!!"

CLAIM your peace with food instead. Declare it. Breathe, then make a 100% commitment to stick to your plan, and recognize that any thought, feeling, image, or impulse suggesting you'll ever break this plan between now and the day you die is Pig Squeal.

ALL DOUBT AND UNCERTAINTY IS PIG ACTIVITY.

HOPE IS PIG ACTIVITY.

Don't hope for it, claim it, know it, be it!

There you have it, the Never Binge Again myth busting philosophy and the associated very practical technique for overcoming food addiction in a nutshell. But there's a LOT more to it, and I go into detail in a humorous, fast, easy read in Never Binge

Again. **The book is available for FREE in Kindle, Nook, and/or PDF format at www.NeverBingeAgain.com and I highly recommend you read it first if you haven't already.** *(Links to paperback and Audible copies are also available but there is a small fee to purchase these).*

Praise for Never Binge Again from Medical Doctors and Therapists

"My life has totally changed. I've lost about 17 pounds. I don't have to carry on the food conversation in my head anymore. It's very clear what my body needs and wants. So as long as I stick with that my weight keeps on dropping three or four pounds per month [...] I can tell you that many of my doctor friends are in trouble with obesity and overeating. It's quite telling to go see another doctor myself as a patient myself and see them struggling with marked obesity problems. I think that doctors need help and would be interested [in Never Binge Again] not only for themselves but for their patients!" - *Margaret Fletcher, M.D. - The first female surgeon ever on the faculty at Johns Hopkins University Medical Center*

"I would really encourage providers to expose their patients to this program because they may very well be surprised to find out that the mindset shift that Never Binge Again offers could be the ticket to really change this patient's life forever. And keep the change sustainable where they don't have to rely on a medicine or some kind of a fad-diet that's going to fail again." *Carmine DiMartino M.D. - Broad Spectrum Family Medicine*

"The majority of my patients are obese or have some obesity complications, people do really want to hear what you have to say, they are devastated by this obesity epidemic [...] and I present Never Binge Again to my patients who really want to change [...] The difference between your program and all the other programs is that NBA really empowers people!" *Susana Thomas M.D. - Family Physician*

"Never Binge again is a very simple mind-hack [...] it is very clear and understandable [...] there are clear action steps to take [...] there's no room for distraction and I really like the humor!" *Dr. Krystyna Grabski, Phd in Cognitive Neuroscience and Cognitive Psychology*

"So much more effective than [the other things I've used with clients]" *Mary, New York State Licensed Social Worker*

Again, the book is available for FREE in Kindle, Nook, and/or PDF format at www.NeverBingeAgain.com and I highly recommend you read it first if you haven't already. *(Again, links to paperback and Audible copies are also available but there is a small fee for purchase).*

OK, with a solid grounding in the Never Binge Again philosophy and method behind us, let's talk about specific binge triggers and how to beat them.

You can use the Binge Trigger Busters section of this book like an index and just look up the triggers that bother you, but please be sure you read the rest in full as it contains several very powerful, crucial motivational thoughts which will help you get through ANY binge eating situation, even those not listed here. Furthermore, reading through ALL the triggers even though you'll naturally be most interested in just a few, will help you discern patterns of thought and behavior which will help with uncommon triggers we may not have listed here.

Last note about a few redundancies you may find in the book – in some situations the solution for multiple triggers is the same. In these cases, you'll notice I've repeated the solution in slightly different words. The reason for this is that some people will ONLY read the trigger sections which apply specifically to their unique situation.

CHAPTER 2: THE REAL NATURE OF BINGE EATING TRIGGERS

As we move into the formal part of this book and begin discussing overeating triggers, it's important to pause for just a moment to talk about causality, because even though the word "trigger" is in common usage and therefore the best title for this book, the word itself can imply a causal element which is NOT there. The point is, NONE of the thoughts, emotions, physical sensations, or environmental stimuli presented in this book can MAKE you overeat in the sense that striking a match on dry wood can trigger a chain reaction which burns down the barn. The triggers can only initiate desire, not behavior...

There is always a chasm between desire and behavior in which your rational mind can choose whether to turn impulse into action.

Binge eating triggers do NOT cause your binges...they cause your desires.

Only YOU can decide to Binge. Only you have control of your hands, arms, mouth, legs, and tongue. Only you can get the car keys, walk to the car, put on your seat belt, start the engine, drive to the store, walk through the aisles, get the Slop your Pig wants, bring it to the counter, take out your wallet, take out the money, hand it to the checkout person, take your change, carry your bags back to the car, find a private place to sneak eat, open the package with your hands, take out the Slop, put it in your mouth, chew, and swallow it.

This might seem like a subtle distinction, but language is VERY important because if you think "XYZ trigger made me binge" you're giving away your power. To get control over your eating, you must resist any notion of powerlessness. You can't abdicate responsibility, even though it would make you feel less guilty. Take the immediate, short term psychological pain associated with having overeaten. It's MUCH better than believing you're subject to the whim of mysterious forces outside of your control, I promise! *(More on managing guilt later).*

CHAPTER 3: EMOTIONAL TRIGGERS AND THEIR BUSTERS

Do you eat for emotional reasons? The relationship between emotional upset and overeating is a little complex. I should know, I studied it for thirty years, even funding my own 40,000-person study on the internet *(in the days when online advertising was VERY cheap!)* One of the things I found was an intriguing connection between the types of food people tended to binge on and specific emotional difficulties. For example,...

- ➢ People who couldn't stop eating chocolate were more likely to be experiencing heartache and/or loneliness...
- ➢ People who couldn't stop binging on salty, crunchy snacks tended to be very stressed at work...
- ➢ People who overdid pasta and bread tended to struggle with anxiety or depression...

Not everyone fit these patterns, but it was noticeable.

Now, since I personally always had a chocolate problem, I investigated this further in my own life. Yes, I was struggling with heartache in a difficult marriage. But more intriguingly, when I told my Mom about the study she said *(paraphrasing)*...

> *"You know Glenn, when you were a toddler your Dad was in the army and we were frightened he was going to be sent to Viet Nam. And your grandfather was missing for 9 months. I was very overwhelmed and depressed, and I couldn't always give you the hugs and love you needed when you came crying to me, so I would give you some chocolate syrup and that always calmed you down!"*

You'd think that would've cured my chocolate problem, but it did NOT. Did it improve my relationship with my Mom? Most definitely. Did it help me feel more compassionate towards myself? Without question. Was it worth investigating? Yes!!

But here's the thing...

EMOTIONAL INSIGHT IMPROVES YOUR LIFE BUT DOES NOT CURE OVEREATING!

Write that on your bathroom mirror and read it every day, because as long as you believe you must overcome all your emotional issues in order to stop overeating you'll just be giving your Inner Food Demon(tm) one more excuse to keep feeding.

See, while emotional issues may have lit the match that started the fire *(and even determined exactly where and what type of fire you're dealing with)*, once it's burning, the fire takes on a life of its own, because the hyper-palatable, industrial food-like-substances people typically binge on *(bags, boxes, bars, containers, etc)* are NOT natural. They did not exist in the tropics as we were evolving and we have NOT been physiologically prepared to deal with the immense toxic pleasure they produce.

In essence, once the fire's been started there is an intense biological craving which has been programmed into your neurology...

A DESIRE TO GET HIGH WITH FOOD WHICH EXISTS INDEPENDENT OF ANY EMOTIONAL CONFLICT YOU MAY BE EXPERIENCING! *(Read that again, it's VERY important!)*

What you need to do most urgently is PUT OUT THE FIRE, not dive into a deep investigation to figure out what started it. You CAN investigate later on to improve your life in other ways, but for God's sake don't get stuck in years of emotional analysis trying to find the burnt match while the fire is devouring your home!

Thankfully, there IS a way to do this, And it's a LOT easier than you think!

HOW TO PUT OUT THE EMOTIONAL EATING FIRE

- **First, stop telling yourself you're overeating for emotional reasons, to comfort yourself, or to relieve stress.** That's a mindset which feeds the fire and gives your Inner Pig™ an excuse. *("We're WAY too upset and these feelings are intolerable - we simply MUST have comfort food to escape them" – Your Pig)*

- **Instead, remind yourself you're binging to get high with food, much like a drug addict might.** This should make it a LOT more uncomfortable to you and take away your inner enemy's favorite excuse. This is a GOOD thing!

- **Tell your Inner Pig you're willing to go through ANY level of emotional discomfort in order to remain binge-free.** Life is not a pain free experience. Accept life on life's terms. Although it may be very uncomfortable at times you won't distract yourself and/or waste your physical and mental energy on recovering from a binge. This energy will then be available to SOLVE the problems you're facing. The only way out is through.

➢ REMEMBER: **If you've got six problems and then you overeat, well, then you'll have seven problems.**

➢ **NONE of this means you've got to get rid of the emotions (or fix the problems they represent) before you can stop overeating.** In fact, it's kind of the opposite. You've got to let your Inner Pig know you're willing to feel any degree of emotional discomfort and STILL stick to your Food Plan. I remember distinctly having to implement this insight the week my Mom got the recurrence of ovarian cancer which killed her 3 months later. That same week I also learned a dear friend had unexpectedly died in his sleep. And I had another rather serious personal struggle with a woman I was dating at the time.

See, life is NOT a pain-free experience. We are not guaranteed happiness just because we stop letting the Pig Binge. What you get when you eliminate Pig Slop from your life is LIFE - for better or for worse. *Marry your life, not your Pig*. It's much better to BE here and be present no matter what emotional pain life brings than to spend days, weeks, or months recovering from Pig Slop. The only way out is through.

➢ **IMAGINE THIS!** You're sitting a dark room, looking through a one-way mirror. On the other side you see the person you love the most in the world: Your child. Or your spouse. Or your parent. They are going about their daily lives, playing, reading, talking to others. But all the while, a man with a Boar's head follows them around, squealing nasty, corrupting things into their ear. "You'll never lose weight!", "It's useless!", "Let's stop playing and go EEEAAATTTTT!!!", "You've tried a thousand times before and never succeeded", "You're a failure", "You're fat – just accept it!"

> What would you do? Would you continue sitting there just watching and doing nothing? Would you tell your child to love this crazy boar-demon and try to reason with it? Or would you get mad to the point your hands shook and you could feel your temples throbbing? Would you go into the other room, scream at the boar demon with all your might and fight it tooth and nail until you locked it in its cage so it could NEVER again harm your child?
>
> I think I know your answer, but my question is, why don't you treat your own Inner Pig the same exact way? Why not harness the same anger you'd feel in the situation above to lock away your own Inner Pig for good, after all, it's just as harmful to you and your family!

Once you get it, REALLY get it, you'll stop letting emotions confuse the issue. You'll still have them, perhaps even more strongly, but you'll understand they don't run the show. You've simply been lying down, drowning in six inches of mud this whole time, when all you ever needed to do was stand up, wash off the muck, and walk away.

It took me 30 years to realize this!

Three utterly wasted decades I'll never get back, and I'd like to save you this pain, because from the bottom of my heart to the bottom of yours I know you CAN do this! So let's go through the specific Emotional Pig Squeals to give you even more strength to combat this insidious delusion.

#1 Low Self Esteem

Low self-esteem is almost always associated with self-critical thoughts.

You might be surprised to learn that overeating/binging actually *requires* negative thinking. In fact, it's very difficult to continue it if you refuse to keep yelling at yourself. That' low-self-esteem and negative thinking are all Binge m Pig activity. What's really going on is the Pig trying to make you feel too weak to resist the next Binge. You can tell for sure it's the Pig generating all this negative activity because as soon as you start to even consider eating some Slop it's tone changes dramatically:

> ➢ "Oooooooh YES!!! You are horrible. Pathetic, really, when it comes right down to it. You'll probably always be fat. When the hell are you going to just give up and accept your fate already? At least then you might enjoy being a happy fat person. Everything totally sucks in our life. Hey, but at least there's ONE good thing: PIG SLOP!!! Yippeee!!! Finally, you're seeing the light!!!" – Your Pig

See what I mean?

Those bad records that get stuck in your head and keep playing over and over again are just your Pig trying to justify eating more Slop.

This is a piercing insight. Once you understand that all negative thinking about food is Pig based and binge motivated, it becomes a lot harder to give it credence.

Here's a related insight that's even more important...

SELF LOVE IS NOT NECESSARY TO STOP OVEREATING! NOR IS ANYONE ELSE'S LOVE!

I DO want you to know, with all my heart and soul, that I WANT you to have love in your life. I WANT you to find more each day. And I WANT you to have wonderful people, family members, spouse, significant others, children, co-workers, friends, etc. who shower you with love.

I BELIEVE IN LOVE...BUT I DO NOT BELIEVE IT IS NECESSARY

TO BE LOVED IN ORDER TO STOP OVEREATING!

Please don't smack me in the head with a spatula, hear me out first! See, as both a psychologist and a coach I've had intimate conversations with literally THOUSANDS of people...so I can tell you definitively there are a LOT of miserable fat people out there. People genuinely going without the love they need. People who do NOT love themselves as they should.

But there also a LOT of miserable thin people. People who are ALSO genuinely without the love they need in their life, and ALSO do not love themselves as they should, but who nevertheless continue to eat healthy! *(Please note I'm NOT talking about people who are thin due to anorexia or bulimia, that's a whole different conversation.)*

Now, this next thought might not be a "feel good" thing which makes me popular with your Mom, but it's critically important nonetheless: It's entirely possible to hate yourself, have a genuinely miserable life, be furious with everyone around you, be horrendously depressed, anxious, etc, ALL these things can be true and you can STILL eat well! And as a matter of fact, if you DO eat well despite all these negative feelings, the odds are much better you'll eventually have the energy to DO something about your life to make it better. Plus, when you consistently SEE yourself taking better care of yourself, you WILL develop more self-love. It's a foregone conclusion!

Of course, your Pig will say I'm full of prairie pooh. "You don't love yourself enough, and nobody is doing it for you. Therefore the ONLY worthwhile pleasure in life is Pig Slop so let's go Binge on some right now!" Well, please tell the Pig it can choke on my sister's ear wax because overeating will only add to your problems. It makes nothing better at all.

The upshot?

Don't wait for love to stop overeating!

Stop overeating so love can find you.

#2 Self Doubt

HOW TO GET OVER ALL THE SELF DOUBT? Simple... don't! Assign it to your Pig instead, and separate your conscious, human identity from it entirely. Since it's your conscious, human identity that controls your hands, arms, legs, mouth and tongue, this gives you the power to decide what, when, and where to eat DESPITE the self doubt.

This is a conscious DECLARATION *(not feeling)* that doubt about your ability to eat well is no longer welcome in your self-concept. "I don't want that, my Pig does. I don't eat Pig Slop and I don't eat from a Pig's Trough. I'm not AFRAID I might eat it, my Pig just really WANTS to eat it!"

#3 Feeling Bored

Does Your Inner Pig(tm) "Make" You Eat When You're Bored?

I've got news for you...

The experience of being bored is NOT the experience of having nothing to do.

It's the painful experience of actively suppressing (and preventing yourself from knowing) your life's purpose!

If you knew your life's purpose, every moment would be precious. Every last one. You'd be making phone calls, writing notes for your book, organizing projects, gathering people around you to move things forward and contribute to the world in the way you most wanted to.

Even if that purpose were "only" to be a better parent, spouse, artist, etc. (There's nothing that says professional pursuits are more valuable.)

Feeling bored is actually a sign that you are pushing through to FIND your life's purpose.

That's it just on the other side of that boredom.

Waiting for you... beckoning.

So when your Pig says you simply MUST eat some Slop because boredom is intolerable, tell it to STFU!

Because you're FED UP with letting it keep you from your purpose.

You're sick and tired of it getting you to live a much smaller life than you deserve!

Sit with the boredom. See what comes. What should you be doing, saying, or being that you aren't now? Who should you be connecting with that, to this point, you've neglected? Where should you be going?

BOREDOM IS WONDERFUL

Embrace it. Walk through it. You just might find yourself on the other side.

Scout's honor! You don't have to believe me, you only need to try it. After all, what if I'm right?

#4 Feeling Deprived

Do you ever feel overwhelmed by feelings of deprivation?

Does your Pig say it's just not fair that you can't eat as much chips, dip, cheese, nachos, chocolate, cake, pizza, pasta, bread, bagels, sugar, flour, oil, and other things that really do taste good, even though you know they're unhealthy?

Or perhaps it says you'll be perceived as too much of a weirdo with your friends and family. Nobody will ever want to eat with you again. You'll be doomed to sit in the corner and eat lunch all by yourself like that no-friends-pimply-faced little kid in the school lunch room when you were a child, right?

There are several ways to overcome this "deprivation trap."

First, remember there are *two* types of deprivation. There's the kind you feel when you don't indulge, but there's also what you deprive yourself of when you *do*. For example, if I never eat a donut again then I'll deprive myself of the mouth feel, taste, and the sugar/flour rush.

There's no getting around this, I will feel this deprivation. However, if I *do* continue eating donuts, I will be depriving myself of all the benefits of *not* eating them! For example, I couldn't live nearly as worry-free regarding diabetes, heart attacks, strokes, and other cardiovascular events. I couldn't sail through my day with the presence of mind, body, and spirit provided by regular, even blood sugar. I couldn't be nearly as confident in my appearance, nor enjoy the energy that comes with having the thin, healthy body I can achieve by abstaining.

It's never a matter of whether you'll feel deprived, it's always a matter of which type of deprivation you'll choose. I'm not arguing that everyone should stop eating donuts. What I am saying is, make your choice in a more fully informed state. Stop to think about what you are giving up in both scenarios, not just the short-term loss of immediate physical pleasure.

Second, tell yourself you're not really giving up that much! Sticking with the same illustration, what am I *really* giving up in the present if I don't eat that donut? The sugar/flour rush only lasts between 18 to 39 minutes and is almost inevitably followed by a crash, which takes hours to recover from. This is associated with a loss of productivity and more difficulty being mindful and present in the world, which influences your relationship with others throughout the day, and downgrades your productivity and accomplishment. More simply put, it's exponentially harder to "seize the day" with a donut in your gut than without!

Third, remind yourself that if you care about the people you're dining with, someone has to go first and be a healthy leader! According to the World Health Organization:

➢ 67.9% of adults are overweight in the United States alone. Worldwide obesity since 1975 has tripled.

➢ Diabetes has increased by 80.8%, and diabetic adults live with double the risk of heart attack and stroke, and a seriously increased risk of blindness and kidney failure. Yet "simple lifestyle measures have shown to be effective in preventing or delaying the onset of type 2 diabetes" – most notably to "achieve and maintain a healthy body weight," "eat a healthy diet," and "be physically active."

➢ Cardiovascular disease is responsible for 31% of global deaths! But "most cardiovascular disease can be prevented by addressing behavioral risk factors—*primarily "unhealthy diet, obesity, and lack of exercise!"*

➢ 30% to 50% of cancers can be prevented, and dietary modification is an important approach to cancer control. "There is a link between overweight and obesity to many types of cancer such as esophagus, colorectum, breast, endometrium and kidney [...] Regular physical activity and the maintenance of a healthy body weight, along with a healthy diet, considerably reduce cancer risk"

It seems our world has made a tacit agreement to support each other in social environments to slowly kill ourselves with food. So look around the table and ask yourself if you genuinely care about any of the people there. If you do, then show them it's possible to resist this social pressure. Because if you don't, who will?

Finally, be sure you are eating enough healthy food. People who struggle with overeating are usually also very good dieters. They tend to restrict their calories and nutrition for periods of time. When you do that, you're signaling your brain that you live in an environment of scarcity. It's only natural then, that when your brain sees calories and nutrition are finally more abundantly available, it will try to get you to hoard them. So, take yourself out of the "feast and famine" cycle and eat plenty of healthy food throughout the day. You'll have a much easier time with the deprivation trap the next time it faces you.

Carpe diem!

References:

➢ Roth, Geneen. (2016, Aug). Reality Bites. [Blog post]. Retrieved from https://geneenroth.com/2016/08/11/realty-bites/

#5 Financial Concerns

Most of my life I was very successful. I was a doctor seeing patients by the time I was 25. I immediately started a parallel career doing advertising consulting for industry. I recall writing a proposal right out of graduate school for more than $50,000. I couldn't believe I got it, and they actually sent the check. In my 30s I built a practice in a NYC suburb doing child and family therapy. I both loved what I was doing and was overloaded with clients within 18 months. Then I invented a research protocol and sold a project based upon it to Bausch and Lomb for about

$1,000,000. You might say I had a Midas touch in my youth.

But when I was 37 that all changed. A drunk driver hit my car and caused an undiagnosed injury that led to a decade of migraines if I worked too long on the computer. And unbeknownst to me I also had undiagnosed Lyme Disease which made treating the migraines next to impossible. Finally, my ex-wife and I had taken the money from the big project and invested it in building the fanciest, most modern, most technologically up to date focus group facility on Long Island. We hired approximately 20 people to run it. We took on a monthly nut of about $150,000.

And then 9/11 happened. We were just outside of NYC. Nobody wanted to fly to New York to do research anymore. Internet streaming was coming into vogue and the big companies took to it like flies to honey. No reason to send their employees across the world anymore to watch focus groups. But we had a 10 year lease, had invested a fortune getting started, and were essentially dead in the water.

That fiasco went on for two years before we got out. We lost everything we had and more. The loss was roughly $2,000,000, and the funny thing about losing $2,000,000 is that it's NOT like losing your car keys. You don't have to HAVE $2,000,000 to lose $2,000,000. We wound up very deep in debt.

In the meantime, I gained a LOT of weight and made myself even sicker looking for solace in pizza, chocolate, and Pop-Tarts *(this was in the pre-Never Binge Again era).*

I became fat, sick, and broke...

When I could've just been broke!

Moreover, I could've handled all the vendors screaming for money, the incredible stress of having to let go of treasured employees, the constant fights with my spouse...

I could've handled it ALL so much better if I were only broke!

Without Pig Slop constantly running through my veins.

And without having to carry the burden of an extra 60 to 80 pounds around with me on top of the money worries.

And you know what? There were NO men in white suits with mustaches who ever came to take away my house, my car, my computer.

Or my *healthy* food options and my treadmill.

And that's the lesson I'd like you to take away!

You don't have to get fat, sick and broke. In fact, if you stay away from Slop you'll have more capability of dealing with the concrete financial issues in the first place! So you probably won't even go broke.

But even if you do, I can tell you from experience it's about a billion times better to be broke vs. fat, sick, and broke. *(It took me a few years to take the weight off for good, and the blood lipid issues interfered with diagnosing the real problem with the migraines)*

There's a FANTASTIC podcast I did about the whole experience of my financial recovery here: https://www.neverbingeagain.com/TheBlog/psychology-of-eating/my-most-listened-to-teleconference-ever/

#6 Feeling Stressed and Overwhelmed

Not infrequently our Pigs will say "OMG there's just too WAY much to handle. We have entirely too many problems, things to do, and places to be. No single human being should ever have to manage so much. It's inhuman. I mean, you can't possibly expect us to go through this without at least a little Slop for comfort can you? How cruel and inhuman can you be!?"

When you step back to think of it however, this Squeal doesn't make any sense because overeating doesn't solve anything. In fact, it only gives you "comfort" *(a food high)* for 18 to 39 minutes before the crash, depending upon the particular junk you choose. Then you're stuck having to recover from the havoc it plays on your blood sugar, digestion, blood pressure, etc. for at least several hours *(if not days.)*

No, eating Pig Slop doesn't solve stressful problems, it creates them.

"If you have six problems and you overeat then you'll have seven problems."

Overeating drains your productivity, creates more overwhelm, and gives you MORE to do.

#7 Feeling Lonely

Many clients report being alone is a REAL "danger time" for food binges. It's a time when all the bags, boxes, and containers of junk seem to hold particularly strong appeal. Some of my clients have become downright frightened of being alone, and even go to great lengths to avoid it entirely!

But here's the thing, being alone is a wonderful time to reflect on and enjoy your progress. Or to mindfully eat some HEALTHY food and cherish every last bite, letting it nourish you body, mind, and soul.

Time alone is when we can journal, set goals, problem solve obstacles, and make plans to move our lives forward.

When we can look at pictures of our loved ones and feel grateful for all they have brought into our lives.

Time alone is when we can develop insights and breakthroughs through deep thought and reflection.

When we can sing aloud, start a new project, take a nap, stare at the dog, or give yourself a hug.

When we're alone we can simply breathe and BE!

But our Inner Pigs say time alone can only be filled with Binges and Pig Slop(tm)...

Screw that noise!!!

I AM with you all during your alone times, ever thinking of better ways to get through and help.

Time alone is precious.

PS - If you really hate being alone, you should know there's no real reason you have to be in today's world. There are literally hundreds of forums where others are happy to chat and support you. Just search Facebook or Google Groups for the subject which interests you most, then reach out and introduce yourself. Or go to Meetups.com and find a group. Loneliness is solvable. Your Pig would love you to think it's not, however, because then it can say "At least we have Pig Slop for company... at least there's that. Can we go get us some right now? Pretty please? PLEEEEEEAZZ!! Oh C'mon!!" The heck with that logic. Go take care of yourself and throw your Pig back into its cage.

#8 Feeling Ashamed

HOW TO OBLITERATE SHAME AND DESPERATION AROUND FOOD: Shame and desperation are two of your Inner Pig's biggest tools. For example, let's say your Inner Pig just found a hole in your Food Plan...

You went out, drank just a tiny bit too much and when you came home the Pig used your inebriated state to start an unimaginable, mind blowing, terrible late night binge :-(

You tossed and turned all night, trying desperately to digest that godawful amount of food.

Got up in the morning after just a few hours of sleep, your stomach aching and bloated, your head throbbing, Barely able to imagine brushing your teeth and taking a shower, let alone getting through the day.

That's about when your Inner Pig should start squealing...

"You're such a failure" - it'll whisper in your ear.

"You're never going to be thin and healthy".

"You're worthless" - it hisses.

"We may as well give up and just be fat and happy".

NONE OF THIS IS TRUE!

See, it's only your Pig's way of setting you up for the next binge.

It's trying to weaken your self-concept to make you feel incapable of resisting. Essentially it's saying: "Life is miserable because you're pathetic but there's always ONE good thing we can do - Binge!"

Here's the point:

Every single insecure, shameful and desperate thought regarding food and eating is only your Pig Squealing it's ass off to set up the next binge.

So WHENEVER you hear those thoughts say "Shut up Pig! I know what you're doing! Get back in your cage!!!"

And either resume the Food Plan which worked best for you or give yourself some thinking time to adjust your plan and prevent the Pig from fooling you again.

#9 Feeling Anxious

It's true that certain foods can help reduce anxiety, but for binge eaters, we really must PLAN them into our diet entirely, not eat them impulsively, because out of control overeating increases anxiety much more so than the reduction you might expect from the food itself. Stick to the Never Binge Again principle of moving your food decisions from your emotions to your intellect! Use one of the online calculators and/or speak with a nutritionist to assess specific nutritional deficits in your own diet.

Foods and nutrients that may MAY help reduce anxiety:

- **Magnesium.** Diets low in magnesium were found to increase anxiety behaviors in mice. Foods rich in magnesium include leafy greens such as spinach and Swiss chard, legumes, nuts, seeds, and whole grains.
- **Regular Blood Sugar:** Don't skip meals or you may feel jittery.
- **Omega 3s from fatty fish like wild salmon.**
- **Priobiotics**: For social anxiety in particular.
- **Antioxidants**: Anxiety is thought to be correlated with a lower overall anti-oxidant state

Another perspective is that eating Slop to quell your anxiety only tells the Pig that you can't handle the anxiety itself, which is the opposite of what you want to do. What you WANT to do is show the Pig you're willing to put up with any level of emotional discomfort in order to stick to your Food Plan. From this perspective, anxiety is an opportunity to make your Inner Pig suffer because it will get all excited about possibilities, then that much more demoralized when you don't feed it. Good!

Here's a paradigm shifter you might consider when you're experiencing anxiety:

"The Nightmare We Fear Most Is the One We've Already Lived Through" - D.W. Winnicott

In my 30+ years working with literally more than a thousand patients and coaching clients, not to mention my own relentless soul searching, journaling, and therapy, this quote from child psychiatrist Donald W. Winnicott about fear is perhaps my favorite. I constantly see people (myself included) obsessing about "what if X happens or Y happens?", when clearly it's the pain of what already HAS happened they are reliving and projecting onto their current circumstances.

- "What if my business fails?" -- when clearly it's the instability and insecurity of a previous environment they are reliving.

- "What if the love of my life leaves me?" - when clearly it's the pain of having been left unloved in the PAST, resurfacing.

- "What if I get some horrible illness and lose my mobility and/ or independence?" - when clearly it's the pain of not having fully lived life to date which ails them.

The problem with all this is that it keeps us living in the past, and can create a self-fulfilling prophesy.

- If you're constantly worried about your business failing, you're draining energy from actually building your business and seeing opportunities right in front of you.

- If you're constantly terrified your love will leave you, you're not fully in the present, connecting with him or her on the deepest level, thereby making it more likely they WILL leave.

- If you're constantly worried about illness, you're sacrificing mental energy which COULD be focused on improving your health and fitness, thereby making you less well than you could be.

What I try to do when I find myself obsessing about a fear is ask myself "How is this most like what I've already been through, and how is it different?"

That usually calms me down enough to get me focused again in the present, on improving my life, and pursuing my goals and relationships.

"The nightmare we fear most is the one we've already been through"

Last, if you suffer from panic attacks, I did a great interview with an expert that has some unusual and counter-intuitive advice you've probably not heard elsewhere. You can listen to it here:

https://www.neverbingeagain.com/TheBlog/uncategorized/coping-with-feelings-of-intense-anxiety-and-panic/

References

➢ *(Naidoo, U. (2016) [Blog Post] Retrieved from https://www.health.harvard.edu/blog/nutritional-strategies-to-ease-anxiety-201604139441)*

#10 Apathy – When You Just Don't Care

WHAT IF YOU JUST DON'T CARE WHETHER YOU OVEREAT OR NOT?

One of the hardest Squeals most people have to deal with is

"F___ it. I just don't care about my stupid Food Plan anymore - let's just let the Pig out!"

This is a variation of the Conscious Pig Party. The solution to it is two fold. Yes, you want to enhance your motivation. Make a list of why you're doing this - the future you're trying to build and read it out loud every day. Create a vision of the future you're trying to avoid too!

But more importantly you need to answer a crazy question for yourself...WHY DO YOU HAVE TO CARE? Why can't there be some things you do to take care of yourself regardless of whether you feel like it or not? Why do you have to be in love with your feelings? Why can't you eat healthy regardless of what you feel?

Personally, I don't care to floss my teeth. I really f-----g hate it. I don't think there's any amount of motivational enhancement which would make me want to do it. I just don't care! But you know what? I do it anyway.

In fact, some people can get themselves to do good things for themselves BECAUSE they don't care.

See, the lie in the Pig Squeal "You don't care so therefore you have to binge" is in the "therefore" part. There WILL inevitably be times you don't care. Indifference is a natural part of recovery. But that's OK, you don't have to care, you only have to do what's right.

Duh! Take that o' Piggy Pig Pig 'o Mine!!

But there's one more important piece of the solution...

REMIND YOURSELF **YOU** CARE, YOUR PIG DOESN'T!

If you really didn't care, you wouldn't have read this far in the book. YOU care deeply but your Pig couldn't care less. The thought “I don’t care” is just the Pig doing what it always does - lying to convince you its thoughts are your own, but they're not! *(A big part of what I do to help people stop overeating is show them how to aggressively separate their own identity from their Pig's nasty thoughts.)*

#11 Sneak Eating

When I was 17 years old my parents went out of town. But before they went they told my 15 year old sister Laurie they didn't want her to have any pizza while they were gone because she was already clogged up with mucus from a cold and they felt the dairy was going to make it worse.

Well, you tell a 15 year old girl NOT to get pizza, what do you think she's gonna do?

Order pizza, of course. *(Duh!)*

So late that Sunday evening just before my parents were about to get home, I was at my friend's house when we got a frantic call from my sister:

"Glenn .... Help! Help! Help! ... The bathroom is all black and charred ... what do I do?"

"What do you mean the bathroom is all black and charred?" I said.

"Glenn, I burned the pizza box in the BATHTUB".

"Why?" I asked.

"To get rid of the evidence" she said.

Why in the world Laurie didn’t just put the darn box in the neighbor's garbage next door I’ll never know, but that’s besides the point.

My sister was sneak eating!

And if your Pig is getting YOU to "sneak eat", what it's really up to is looking for an opportunity to shame and guilt you.

Because, you see, shame and guilt will wear your down. And your Pig desperately WANTS to wear you down So you'll feel too weak to restrain its stupid urges.

It took me a LONG time to realize this!

Excessive guilt and shame is almost always Binge motivated!

The whole purpose of holding onto them is so your Pig can convince you that you're a pathetic person with no ability to refrain from eating anything that tastes good. So you might as well give up and accept being a "happy fat person". Or that you don't deserve to be thin.

Or anything else it can tell you to convince you to go feed it some crap!

So if YOU are sneak eating, what you want to do is ask yourself WHY?

Why can't I *(or won't I)* eat this in front of other people?

Sneak eating is a clear signal you need to evaluate your Food Plan.

You should feel perfectly comfortable and accepting about EVERYTHING you're eating when it's 100% on YOUR Plan.

And perfectly willing to eat it in front of ANYONE!

That way your Pig can't wear you down with guilt and shame and make you feel too weak to resist the next Binge.

Sneak eating is like your Food Plan's "check engine" light. If you notice you're doing it, ask yourself if you REALLY believe in your Food Plan 100% and adjust it until you do. Then eat with joy and free of shame!

#12 Feeling Powerless

You can overcome virtually ANY binge eating problem as long as you don't make ONE cardinal sin. Do you know what that is? It's pretending you're powerless over food, as if there was...

> "Some mysterious force which overtakes you, essentially knocking you unconscious and getting you to get in your car, take the keys out of your pocket, start the car, pull it out of the driveway, drive to the store, find a parking spot, take the keys out of the car, walk into the store, select the binge food your Pig wants in the right amount and variety, walk to the cash register, wait on line, put the binge food on the checkout counter, take your wallet out of your pants and/or purse, take out your credit card or cash, make small talk with the cashier, sign for the order, take the bags into the car, open the package with your hands, take the first bite out of the package and put it in your mouth, chew, and swallow."

Prairie Pooh! At every step along the way you CAN intervene to stop the episode. Your Pig would love you to believe you can't. It doesn't want you to notice that every step along the way is a lever you can pull the other way.

It says you're powerless. Diseased. A helpless little child in the face of those bags, boxes, and containers some big profiteer in a white suit with a mustache has so kindly placed in the store for your Pig.

Resolve right here and now NEVER to pretend you're powerless over food. No matter whether you've felt out of control for five hours, five days, or five years, you CAN take back the reigns and stop this train wreck.

You can reverse direction.

You can declare yourself 100% confident that YOU are in control, and decide exactly what healthy vs. binge food and/or behavior is for YOU personally.

Then listen for your Pig trying to convince you to break and ignore that stupid creature.

The notion of powerlessness IS the disease.

If you'd like to squelch the voice of powerlessness and live the rest of your life without the binge eating monster riding your back, then consider joining the NBA Unlimited Coaching and Intensive Training Program.

#13 Intuitive Eating

There are essentially three philosophies one can use to approach eating problems:

> ➢ **Never Binge Again**: NBA is a rules-based approach which says you should draw clear, bright lines between healthy and unhealthy food/food-behaviors and swear off the unhealthy ones forevermore. That doesn't mean there's anything in particular you can't eat, but you always need to know exactly where the bullseye begins and ends *(e.g. "I will only ever eat chocolate again on Saturdays")* because if you don't know where you're going, you'll wind up somewhere else. Then you use these bright lines to separate your thinking into constructive vs. destructive food thoughts, and choose to identify entirely with the constructive thoughts, forevermore ejecting thoughts which might prevent you from sticking to your plan into a fictitious entity we call "The Pig" *(or any other moniker which doesn't make you want*

to cuddle and nurture it.) In so doing you can purge your mind of doubt and distraction so you can focus all your energy on the goal. If you make a mistake you take it seriously, analyze what went wrong, make adjustments if need be, and then forgive yourself with dignity. You eat intuitively within the boundaries of your rules, just like you drive intuitively between red lights and stop signs. Finally, you cultivate confidence that YOU are in control of how your bodily desires are expressed. *(Note: Most other diets and programs are rules-based approaches too: Point counting, calorie counting, etc)*

➢ **Intuitive Eating**: Intuitive eating suggests you eschew any "rules which might distinguish healthy vs. unhealthy eating" and instead focus on your body's intuitive sense of what it needs, at what times, and in what amounts. They suggest that any type of restriction of food causes a binge and is also responsible for the degradation in self-esteem many binge eaters experience. They bill themselves as NOT being a diet—in fact the exact opposite—and is about learning to eat outside of the diet mentality. Intuitive eaters are supposed to give themselves permission to eat as much as they want of whatever they want without feeling guilty. They suggest that recovery is achieved by rejecting the diet mentality, honoring your hunger, making peace with food, challenging the "food police", learning to feel your fullness, focusing on satisfaction, learning to cope with emotions without using food, respecting your body *(stop judging it)*, engaging in movement (exercise) that feels good to you rather than that you feel you "should" be doing, and honoring your health by considering how foods make you feel.

➢ **12 Step Approach**: The 12 step approaches of Overeaters Anonymous, Food Addicts Anonymous, etc. believe that overeating is a disease of "irresistible impulse" and that the addict is powerless to do anything about it by

> themselves. They also suggest one requires lifelong meetings several times per week, dependency upon a sponsor, the cultivation of fear of the impulse, a deep moral inventory and the making of amends, and the necessity of proselytizing the 12-step philosophy to others.

Never Binge Again can be integrated with Intuitive Eating principles if you're willing to consider intuitively eating "between the lines" you set down using Never Binge Again rules. This is very similar to how you drive intuitively between red lights and stop signs. You aren't constantly thinking of the rules of the road, you just "know" them and otherwise rely on your instincts.

That said, Never Binge Again asserts that our hunger meters have been purposefully diverted (and often broken) by all of the hyperpalatable concentrations of starch, sugar, fat, salt, and excitoxins engineered by the food industry's research scientists and multimillion dollar budgets... as well as the advertising industry's money and expertise in making us think we need these things to live.

If things were as they were 100,000 years ago when we all lived in the tropics without all the bags, boxes, and containers, nobody would need Never Binge Again rules and Intuitive Eating would be the defacto best choice. But in today's world we face a constant onslaught of toxic-pleasure which evolution never prepared us to handle, and we require a rules-based, well thought through defense in order to prevail.

If you're very taken with the notion of Intuitive Eating and it's interfering with your progress, ask yourself if "intuitive smoking" makes any sense? There are some things which don't belong in our body. And when it's perfectly legal for the food industry to slip flavored cardboard into our food system (I've actually seen this example), doesn't someone have to stand up and say that drawing clear, bright lines between healthy vs. unhealthy food is not only a good idea but a *necessity?*

I recorded to full length discussions about the intersection and disparities between Intuitive Eating and Never Binge Again you might like to listen to here:

- ➢ https://www.neverbingeagain.com/TheBlog/psychology-of-eating/intuitive-eating-vs-never-binge-again/
- ➢ https://www.neverbingeagain.com/TheBlog/uncategorized/intuitive-eating-part-two/

Never Binge Again is utterly incompatible with the 12 Step philosophy on every single point except the necessity of having a well-defined food plan.

The 12 step people insist you can't control yourself and must fear the impulse to overeat. They say you are abnormal and have a chronic, progressive, and mysterious disease, and must therefore remain dependent upon their program for a lifetime. Never Binge Again, in contrast, suggests your only problem is a healthy appetite which has been utterly corrupted by industry, and the failure to mount the necessary defense, which anyone can do in a short period of time. *(For more on the problems with the 12 step approach please see the next trigger.)*

Generally speaking you will have trouble integrating NBA with either of the other two approaches, except in the manner specifically designated above, because the foundational principles fundamentally conflict and cancel each other out.

I'm not saying it's not possible to succeed using the other approaches or that I've got the only effective one... I'm saying it's best if you DECIDE which one you're using and work hard to make that your primary belief system or else you'll likely struggle.

#14 Twelve Step Mythology

WHAT'S WRONG WITH 12 STEP FOOD PROGRAMS? (Opinion)

I get a LOT of people in my programs who've had trouble succeeding LONG TERM in 12 Step Food Programs. In fact, I personally was one of them and I used to think that was entirely MY problem, but I don't think this (at all) anymore.

But before I tell you why, I just want to say that I know it DOES work for some people. If you happen to be one of them, you might not want to read any further in this section, or at minimum, proceed at your own risk, because the LAST thing I want to do is ruin your success.

That said, here's what I think is dreadfully wrong with the 12 step programs where food addiction is concerned:

(1) The twelve step programs, including the food addiction programs, universally assert addiction is a disease, not a choice. There is essentially NO evidence for this. What's typically presented is a brain scan which shows neurological changes in addicts. What they fail to mention is that these same neurological changes are seen whenever people repeatedly seek pleasure from virtually ANY activity. For example, taxi drivers have been shown to have the same changes. Is taxi-driving a disease? Are taxi-drivers powerless to resist their urge to drive and pick up passengers? Is there really such a thing as a “compulsive taxi driver?”

Speaking as a lay person and NOT a psychologist because what I'm about to say may go against the standards of care for my licensed profession, I firmly believe overeating is NOT caused by a chronic, progressive, mysterious disease which does push-ups in the closet even when you are being good. Instead, I believe your problem is caused by:

- The mistaken belief that industrially produced, hyperpalatable poison is actually a food treat.

- Billions of dollars spent by Big Food to produce an artificially concentrated form of pleasure for which evolution has not prepared us.
- Packaging research to dress up these poisons into something that mimics the way healthy food is supposed to look in nature.
- Billions more in advertising to make it all look "irresistible".
- Even more billions funneled through the addiction treatment industry which has a stake in making you believing you are powerless to stop.
- And most importantly, the failure to recognize and control the intervening thoughts and feelings between stimulus and action. That "little voice" in your head which says "Gimme the Junk" with all sorts of seemingly good reasons at the time of impulse.

The good news is, you don't need "treatment" for a non-existent disease. You just need to clarify exactly where you believe the line is between healthy vs. unhealthy food so you can finally hear that voice inside and learn to coldly ignore it while you continually intake enough healthy nutrition!

(2) The twelve step programs assert that the addict is powerless to resist the impulse to indulge. "There is no power on earth which will help them resist!" *(paraphrasing from the Big Book).* As a result, they're taught to cultivate fear of their own bodies rather than mastery over their impulses. Which leads to a progressive lowering of self-efficacy and self-esteem. This, in my experience, has translated to lesser accomplishment and overall satisfaction with life in my clients.

(3) The implications of the disease model are fierce. People are taught they are abnormal and must sacrifice a great deal of their lives to hanging around with other addicts who also assert they have a mysterious, chronic, progressive disease from which they could suffer a relapse at ANY time. This leads to a long-term sense of depression and anxiety, because 12 steppers always have "that next binge" hanging over their heads. In fact they're taught that confidence is dangerous when in my experience the exact opposite is true!

(4) Twelve step programs encourage dependency. You're supposed to act like a child and sacrifice your autonomy to a sponsor because (according to the program) you're incapable of managing your life like a normal adult. So make yourself dependent upon someone else who says they can't solve the problem on their own - and who asserts without evidence that you can't quit because you've got a disease they've got no proof exists.

(5) Twelve step programs pounce on people who are very vulnerable and searching for help to quit overeating and tell them they CAN'T do it. Then they begin to talk to them in parables and mysteries which distort logic and strain reason. For many of these people, it may have been the one and only moment they were really ready to make a change but they're getting the exact opposite advice they need in my not-so-humble-big-hairy-opinion!

(6) Twelve step programs emphasize "one day at a time, insecure abstinence." In the 12 step programs you'll constantly hear the slogan "one day at a time - I might Binge tomorrow, but for today I choose not to." While this may work to PUT OFF a binge for a while, I believe it's a serious mistake which ultimately makes things worse.

As is so often the case, there IS an important HALF-TRUTH in the 12-step notion. That's what makes it so seductive. The answer to many Pig Squeals indeed IS focusing on the present moment. But the *"you can't possibly know what you'll do tomorrow"* part of the Squeal puts a VERY dark cloud over your head, and keeps it there indefinitely as if it's just a matter of time before the next "involuntary" episode. And this is the general philosophy of the 12 step programs. They cultivate FEAR, when what you SHOULD be cultivating is CONFIDENCE.

What I suggest instead *(thanks to Jack Trimpy at Rational Recovery for this)* is to say "I Never Binge Now", and because it will ALWAYS be now, I am 100% confident I WILL NEVER BINGE AGAIN! See, the future is just an infinite string of NOWs. As you read the words in this sentence, it is now. As you get to the next comma, and this one too, and even this one, it is STILL now. When we arrive at the next paragraph together it will still be now. See? It's NOW again, isn't it!? In fact, tomorrow it will be now again. And next week. And on April 24th, 2072.

IT IS ALWAYS NOW!

So if you truly can never binge NOW, and just keep doing that, you can be 100% confident you will never binge again! You do NOT have to assert you are a helpless, quivering little creature, powerless to face tomorrow, just hoping against hope that some mysterious higher power will save you from yourself. You can be confident that tomorrow it will be now again, and baby, you've got now covered! Develop confidence. Cultivate hope and enthusiasm. Think optimistically. Take responsibility for NOW and stop fearing your own bodily impulses.

When people are ready to do something with their lives they generally need a shot of CONFIDENCE, CLARITY, FOCUS, AND MOTIVATION ENHANCEMENT... not a bunch of unproven gobble-de-gook in a feel good "everyone loves you no matter what" environment.

I mean look, I'm a compassionate guy, really I am. If you need a hug, well, I'm just a big teddy bear. Ask anyone that knows me. But if you want me to lie to you and tell you that you really can't control yourself, if you want me to tell you the best you can ever hope to do is quit abusing yourself with food for a little while, if you want me to make up cockamamie excuse to help you avoid facing what you know in your heart of hearts you've GOT to do about your food problem...

Well, I'm NOT your guy because that's all a bunch of prairie pooh in my not-so-humble-big-hairy-opinion. *(Seriously)*

From the bottom of my heart to the bottom of yours I know YOU can fix your food problem. And really, so you do you, RIGHT?

CHAPTER 4: PHYSICAL TIRGGERS AND THEIR BUSTERS

#15 Binge Eating When Already Full, No Longer Hungry, or Feeling Out of Control with Food

The idea that being too full could be a binge eating trigger seems counterintuitive, to say the least. Yet for countless overeaters this most definitely IS the case! It doesn't make sense until you place it in context.

See, most binge eaters aren't only addicted to overeating, they're addicted to over-*dieting* too. By alternately binge eating *and* desperately trying to make up for it with various forms of fasting and/or over-restricting calories and nutrients, they keep their bodies in a "feast or famine" emergency mode at virtually all times.

When your brain thinks it lives in an environment where it believes it may have to go for long periods of time at any moment without access to vital food and nutrients, it only makes sense that it would say "we'd better HOARD food now" the moment there is any signal which suggests the harvest is here and calories/nutrition is once again available.

Being too full is one such signal, for how could you get that way if food weren't abundant at the moment?

The solution is NOT some magic mantra you repeat at the moment you feel the urge to binge because you ate a little too much already (although you can say "feelings aren't facts" and resist the biological urge).

The solution to "too full" binge eating is to take yourself OUT of the feast and famine mentality by supplying a regular, reliable, steady supply of calories and nutrients to your body so your brain doesn't "panic" and try to hoard food.

That means you need to eat breakfast the day after a binge.

And the next day, and the next, and the next.

If you need to lose weight then calculate a SMALL caloric deficit using one of the nutritional calculators online (I like Cronometer.com) and/or consulting with a licensed dietician or other medical professional. Generally speaking I find if people aren't losing more than a pound or two per week they can more easily manage the impulse to binge when they feel too full. *(I prefer the one pound range).*

The last thing you may want to consider is that there IS a high associated with both the overeating AND the dieting part of the feast and famine cycle. So part of what you'll have to get used to is a more even, contented kind of energy rather than the manic roller coaster you've been keeping yourself on by alternatively binging and restricting.

I hope that makes sense.

Then there is the feeling that one is out of control so therefore the Pig is free to do what it wants to, at least until the end of the day. "You made a mistake and therefore you're totally out of control… and I'm completely free to eat whatever I want until tomorrow. Yippeee!!! YIPPEEE!!! Party time!! Let's do it… let's do it NOW!!" – Sincerely, Your Pig

But when you think of it, that's just silly:

- ➢ If an archer misses the bullseye (s)he doesn't just say "oh well, might as well just shoot the rest of the arrows into the audience.
- ➢ If a hiker slips and falls, they don't think "Hmmmm, I fell. Might as well just roll down the mountain all the way to the bottom or further. Everything's ruined now!"
- ➢ If you chip a tooth, you don't go grab a hammer to bang the rest of them out.
- ➢ If you can't get the answer right to one question on a test you don't just take random guesses and/or purpose-fully screw up the rest.
- ➢ If you accidentally touch a hot stove you don't slam your whole hand down on it and say "Forget it, I'm just a pathetic hot stove toucher – there's no hope for me!"
- ➢ When a baseball pitcher walks a player he doesn't simply start throwing the rest of his pitches into the dugout.
- ➢ If you get a speeding ticket you don't say "F it, might as well ignore ALL the traffic laws from now on – it's pedal to the metal time for me!"
- ➢ If you hit a ball into the net in tennis you don't say "Screw it, I'm just gonna slam them all into the net now because I suck at this game."
- ➢ If you forget your wife's birthday you don't say "That's it, that woman's NEVER getting another card from me again!"
- ➢ If you're late to work one day you don't say "Screw it, I might as well just quit my job!"

- ➢ If you accidentally stub your toe you don't go put your foot in a vice and crank down hard.

- ➢ If you drop your kid off late to school you don't tell him "I guess you don't have to go anymore, too bad, so sad!"

- ➢ If your dog does #2 in the house you don't say "I guess this is where you go #2 from now on."

See what I mean?

If your Pig gets out of its Cage, just put it back.

Analyze how it happened and make any necessary adjustments to your plan.

But for God's sake, just put it back, forgive yourself with dignity, and then commit with perfection once again!

#16 Feeling Too Hungry

I was once at dinner with a group of friends and a man I just met became very angry with me when he found out I'd written a book about weight loss. "Look!", he said as he slammed his palm down on the table. "No matter what you f-----g diet doctors say I do NOT eat because I want to be fat, I eat because I'm f----g hungry!!!"

Feeling too hungry is unquestionably a trigger for many, if not most overeaters. "We're starving! You simply must break this stupid diet or we'll surely die!" says the inner Food Demon. "Just start again tomorrow." Before you know it your best laid plans are out the window and you're burying your face in your favorite bag, box, or container.

But it doesn't have to be this way.

First, accept that your experiential hunger meter may be

broken and make an *objective* assessment. The food industry pushes artificially engineered concentrations of starch, sugar, fat, salt, and excitotoxins that hit our bliss point without giving us enough nutrition to feel satisfied. There are billions of dollars of research that go into ensuring we don't know when to stop, and don't want to even when we do! So forgive yourself for struggling with hunger that is out-of-sync with how many calories you're consuming. This is by design. Instead, make a more factual assessment of whether you do or don't need more food (and what type) by consulting with a licensed dietitian, nutritionist, and/or tallying your calories using any of the free services available online. *(For example Cronometer.com or MyFitnessPal.com)* Do you realistically need more food right now?

Second, unless a doctor is instructing you otherwise, make sure you're not trying to lose weight too quickly. In my experience, people who lose more than one or two pounds a week eventually gain it all back and more. That's because they're not just struggling with overeating, they're struggling with *over-dieting* too. The keep their body stuck in a feast-or-famine cycle where it thinks nutrition and calories are often very scarce, so as soon as they are available the brain says "hoard all you can!"

Once you're objectively sure you don't authentically need more food, here's how to avoid overeating when you feel too hungry:

➢ **Enjoy your hunger!** If you're going to lose weight there are realistically going to be times when you feel hungry, so it's best to learn to enjoy it. This is when your body is turning to stored fat instead of available food. It's a good sign, and a necessary part of trimming down. Tolerating hunger in the context of an authentically nourished body also means you are learning to master your impulses rather than continuing to be their slave.

➢ **Grab your stomach, tush, or hips and say "Let it burn, baby, let it burn!"** Listen, for too long you've been carrying around on your body that extra lunch, dinner, and/or desert. So relish in the fact it's coming off you now. Feel it in the moment. Shout "Let it burn!"

➢ **Tell yourself they're not going to find your bones by the refrigerator!** It takes weeks *(or even months)* for a well-nourished body to starve to death. And while I don't recommend skipping meals if you can avoid it, unless you're seriously underweight and/or anorexic, the likelihood of a News story coming out next week with a video of your skeleton reaching for the refrigerator in a last desperate attempt to avoid starvation are slim to none, right? If you're going to get on a slow and steady plan to shed the inches, you're going to have to learn to enjoy your hunger sometimes. It's a sign of mastery, a sign your body's doing exactly what it's supposed to do: burn the excess weight for fuel instead of the bags, boxes, and containers your Pig says you can't live without. C'mon, they're not going to find your bones by the refrigerator, are they? They certainly won't find mine! So grab those extra inches and chant along with me, won't you? "Let it burn, baby, let it burn! "

➢ **Remember: "Feelings aren't facts!"** The whole point of evaluating things factually is to understand that even though every bone in your body feels like someone better hand over the chocolate or you may finally "go postal", in reality there's nothing at all wrong with not eating any right now. Remember, feelings aren't facts.

➢ **Slow down and think about whether the feeling of hunger comes from your belly or your head.** If you think you have to eat but the feeling doesn't come from your belly, then you should ignore it like the 'Food Demon Squeal' it is! Plus, if it's just a general feeling of fatigue, unease, or discomfort, it might be you're just dehydrated. Try drinking a glass of water and waiting five minutes to see how you feel.

There you have it – some practical strategies to stop overeating when you feel too hungry!

#17 Being Too Tired

Fatigue is no fun! Many of us are able to maintain our diets for the majority of the day, only to lose it when we become too tired and/or physically exhausted.

This is not our imagination either, there are countless studies which suggest that willpower dwindles as we make decisions throughout the day and is further degraded by physical fatigue. Moreover, sleep deprivation and fatigue tend to increase levels of Ghrelin, the "let's eat" hormone. In fact, people who get 4 or fewer hours of sleep per night may consume as much as 22% more calories per day on average!

The first thing to do when you realize you're experiencing "fatigue cravings" is to take a time out. Stop making decisions. Stop trying to be productive. Take a deep breath. Step away from any and all "input" *(people, places, and things which want something from you)* for at least five minutes. Take another breath. Say "I always use the present moment to be healthy." Take another breath.

Second, utilize standard delay tactics. Rather than running to buy and/or eat what you're craving, write it down. Include the specific type of food you're craving, where you would get it, and how much of it would it take to satisfy you. Take another breath.

Then project yourself into the future about 30 minutes *after* you finished eating it. What do you see? How does the future you feel? How's your digestion? Your self-esteem and emotional outlook on things? Take another breath.

Now ask yourself what you could eat that would change that future picture for the better. Specifically where would you get it, how much would you have, and how would you feel afterwards? Take an even deeper breath and sigh it all out.

In addition to this technique you can also take preventative measures. For example, if you didn't get enough sleep and/or know you're going to have an exhausting day, try extra hard to make all your food decisions in the morning when your willpower is strongest. Pack up your food in Tupperware and baggies and have it all sitting and waiting for you later when you know you'll be fatigued.

And consider a rule which says "I will never go to bed again without writing down a hypothetical food plan for the next day." Even though the plan is hypothetical and you have the right to flexibly change it if you need to, the act of thinking it through and writing it down forces you to see any upcoming trouble spots and allows you to plan for same.

Last – try to get more sleep, I know it's easier said than done but it's important!

References

- Blay, Libby. (2016, September 9th). [Blog post]. Retrieved from https://fitmo.com/personal-trainer-blog/stop-food-cravings-tired-hungry/

#18 That Time of the Month

Research suggests that compulsive eating and body dissatisfaction are elevated when progesterone levels rise during the premenstrual phase of your cycle. Moreover, appetite rises when estrogen levels are lowest, which so happens to be during your cycle (they are highest during ovulation). In other words, before and during your period you are physiologically predisposed to be unhappy with yourself and want to devour food!

On the other hand, your metabolism appears to be slightly higher during the luteal phase just before your period due to increased thyroid function.

All things considered it can be helpful to create a conditional rule which allows 5% to 10% extra nutrition and calories *(not junk)* during your time of month. Foods which contain magnesium such as spinach, avocado, and/or black beans... and B6 rich foods such as carrots, peas, bananas, and chickpeas can be particularly helpful because they may boost your serotonin levels and lessen the severity of the cravings. Other credible authors have also suggested eating 30g to 35g of non-fruit carbohydrates (e.g. quinoa and other whole grains) can similarly boost serotonin levels. As always, check with your doctor before changing your diet.

Notwithstanding the above, remember that your Food Rules remain in force regardless of how your Pig feels about them. As much as your Pig may be screaming "just hand over the chocolate and nobody gets hurt", remember that's only a feeling, and feelings are NOT facts. Think through exactly how you want to behave around food during your menstrual cycle beforehand, when you aren't hungry, are well rested, and are at your best. Put it all down in black and white and treat it like law.

References

➢ Racine, S.E., Culbert, K.M., Keel, P.K., Sisk, C.L., Burt, S.A, Klump, K.L. (2011). Differential associations between ovarian hormones and disordered eating symptoms across the menstrual cycle in women. International Journal of Eating Disorders *(Vol 45, Issue 3, 333-334)*

➢ Wurtman, J.J. (2010). You Can Prevent PMS from Destroying Your Diet. [Blog post] Retrieved from https://www.psychologytoday.com/us/blog/the-antidepressant-diet/201008/you-can-prevent-pms-destroying-your-diet

#19 Slow Metabolism

Is "Slow Metabolism Syndrome" preventing you from losing weight?

In one of the weight loss groups my business partner has belonged to over the years
there was this one guy *(let's call him Joe)* he distinctly remembers. Joe was BIG, only 5' 6" but 275 pounds, and even though Joe did everything right, he couldn't lose weight. Every meeting they'd go over his food journal *(which he kept meticulously)* and every time he reported eating EXACTLY according to plan. Joe was also exercising 4-5 times a week, verified by the group moderator who did her daily walks in the same park where he rode his bike.

The moderator started him on a 2,200 calories/day plan. Then took him down to 2,000, and then to 1,800. At which point, he should've been losing several pounds a week, but he didn't shed a single one. Finally, the moderator recommended he test his metabolic rate, and Joe happily obliged her *(even though the test was expensive).*

And...

NOTHING!

His metabolism was perfectly normal. In the group's desperation *(they we're all emotionally invested in Joe's weight loss at this point because he was trying SO hard),* they went through his food journal line by line one last time and my business partner kept asking him "Are you sure you didn't eat more? Are you SURE?"

And then Joe blurted out "Well, I guess might've put more peanut butter on the toast than I should have."

The room went silent. There was NO peanut butter anywhere on the food plan! And it turned out that “a little peanut butter” wasn’t the only “little cheat” Joe was indulging in. In fact, Joe had been binge eating the whole time, but his Pig told him it "didn't count" because it was just "a little something extra", which Joe therefore kept secret!

Well, there's another secret I want to tell you.

Perhaps THE real secret to weight loss.

The secret ingredient to success is NOT the super-special-amazing diet you choose.

It's your ability to follow it!

I’m not saying there’s no such thing as a slow metabolism, but by far my experience with clients is that they’re eating more than they think. So before you diagnose yourself with the slow metabolism curse, methodically go through what you are eating with the idea the EVERYTHING COUNTS. Your Pig desperately wants to convince you that a little of this and a little of that doesn’t matter, but it really does. Because an extra 120 calories per day adds up to about a pound each month. And even just 60 calories/day (1/2 pound per month) mounts the fat on your waist, thighs, or hips when you consider it’s sustained month after month after month. At the very least, it can stop you from losing weight.

But OK, suppose you DO have a slowed metabolism. Here are some legitimate factors to consider changing with the advice of your doctor and/or licensed dietitian:

➢ **All calories are not equal.** There’s research which indicates, for example, that a higher percentage of calories from whole fruits and vegetables is burned as energy vs. stored as fat. Empty calories are more likely to get deposited on your body. Moreover, if your diet is replete with empty calories, your body is somewhat malnourished, and it only makes sense that it would want to hold onto reserves because you're signaling it that enough nutrients aren't consistently available.

➢ **Certain medications can slow your metabolism**: Ask your doctor if your antidepressants, diabetes medication, steroids, and/or hormone therapy might be the culprit and see if (s)he might be willing to adjust them to help with weight loss. Don't take it on yourself to do this please, however, as this can be dangerous. And sometimes just changing the time of day you take your medication can help.

➢ **Hypothyroidism and other health conditions**: Your thyroid isn't the only authentic health condition which could be slowing your metabolism. Check with your doctor.

➢ **Over-restriction**: Eating too little can actually slow your metabolism. Going through periods of severe caloric and/or nutritional deficits signals the body it's got to make do with less. It only makes sense. Between this and the fact that for binge eaters in particular, going through the "famine" part of the feast and famine cycle seems to tell the brain that as soon as food is genuinely available (e.g. you break your diet even a little bit) it should hoard all it can because it never knows when the next famine is coming.

For this reason I find the solution for binge eaters is regular, sustained nutrition throughout the day, day in and day out, at a small caloric deficit... NOT fasting or even intermittent fasting. (At least not for the first six months to a year that they are recovering from overeating. Once you're solidly on your plan and approaching your goal weight I do understand there are medical benefits to fasting, etc. But binge eaters don't seem to have the capacity to go through these periods without a rebound binge that does even more damage – at least not in my experience with them.

➢ **It's Too Warm Where You Live**: In the *Journal of Clinical Endocrinology & Metabolism* several respected researchers reported that a small reduction in ambient temperature at night could as much as double the activity of brown adipose tissue, a type of fat which burns calories rather than stores them. "Brown fat becomes more active in cooler temperatures to help keep us warm," explains Aaron Cypess, an endocrinologist. He suggests you turn down the heat, sleep in cooler temperatures, and spend more time outdoors.

➢ **Lack of Exercise**: If you don't exercise you create conditions which are more likely to allow fat to build up in your body. Regular exercise, and particularly aerobic interval training, seems to boost metabolism

➢ **Not Drinking Enough Water**: If you don't drink enough water the odds are the liquids you are drinking may be filled with empty calories, which in turn slow your metabolism (see above).

➢ **Not Getting Enough Sleep**: Less than sufficient sleep has been shown to increase levels of the hunger hormone ghrelin while reducing levels of the fullness hormone leptin. It also increases cortisol levels which can cause you to store more fat. Gotta get your Zzzzs!

References

➢ Davy, B.M, Dennis, E.A., Dengo, A.L, Wilson, K.L., and Davy, K.P. (2008). Water consumption reduces energy intake at a breakfast meal in obese older adults. Journal of the American Dietetic Association, Jul;108(7):1236-9. doi: 10.1016/j.jada.2008.04.013 https://www.ncbi.nlm.nih.gov/pubmed/18589036

- Kong Y. Chen Robert J. Brychta Joyce D. Linderman Sheila Smith Amber CourvilleWilliam Dieckmann Peter Herscovitch Corina M. Millo Alan Remaley Paul Lee, Francesco S. Celi (2013). Brown Fat Activation Mediates Cold-Induced Thermogenesis in Adult Humans in Response to a Mild Decrease in Ambient Temperature. The Journal of Clinical Endocrinology & Metabolism, Volume 98, Issue 7, 1 July 2013, Pages E1218–E1223

- Stodard, G. (2018, November). Changing Your Metabolism Isn't Complicated or Mysterious. [Blog post] Retrieved from https://tonic.vice.com/en_us/article/mbya73/changing-your-metabolism-isnt-complicated-or-mysterious

- https://www.everydayhealth.com/weight-pictures/triggers-that-will-slow-your-metabolism.aspx#lack-of-exercise-can-slow-metabolism

#20 Feeling Thirsty

Feeling thirsty isn't generally a trigger in and of itself for binge eating *(contrary to popular opinion the research doesn't seem to indicate people confuse hunger and thirst)*, but that doesn't mean you should let yourself get dehydrated. There are about a zillion other reasons to drink enough water during the day, and these reasons may indeed put you back in your right mind when you feel like binging. So before you give in to the impulse to overeat, try drinking some water, probably a lot of it. It just might do the trick.

What are those reasons?

Staying hydrated has a major impact on energy levels and brain function–even mild dehydration in the 1% to 3% range of body weight can often impair brain function. Just a 1.3% fluid loss has also been shown to impair mood in women, and 1.6% is shown to increase anxiety and fatigue in men, as well as diminishing working memory.

So drink up for your mood, energy, peace of mind, and memory!

References

➢ McKierman, F, Hollis, JH, Mattes, RD (2009). Thirst-drinking, hunger-eating; tight coupling? J Am Diet Assoc. 2009 Mar;109(3):486-90.

➢ Leech, J (2017, June). 7 Science-Based Health Benefits of Drinking Enough Water. [Blog Post]. Retrieved from https://www.healthline.com/nutrition/7-health-benefits-of-water

#21 Feeling Fat

When you've got some weight to lose, particularly if you're feeling a little bloated after a Binge, your Pig will insist you've got to lose it FAST! "This is totally unacceptable!!!" your Pig will shout, *"One or two pounds a week is crap! We'll never get to our goal at that rate. It's just AWFUL being fat. Nothing fits. It's so uncomfortable. We can't move like we used to, wear the sexy dresses and jeans we used to, or even go out with our friend like we used to. We need to just stop eating or go on a ridiculously low-calorie diet so that this fat just melts off us like butter on a 100 degree day!! Of course, we know that's going to be impossible too because it'll make us want to binge, so why don't we just cut to the chase and binge binge binge binge BINGE!! Can we? Can we, can we, can we, huh? Pretty pleaz!!!??" – Your Pig*

Listen, I know this is hard to accept when you've got a Squealing Pig to contend with but...

The fastest way to lose weight is slowly.

You might want to write that on the inside of your eyelids, that's how important it is. *(Note: Don't really do that or my neurotic lawyer will have a fit.)*

I've seen it a thousand times. So many, in fact, that I literally cringe when people tell me they're losing more than 2 pounds per week *(except for the very first week)* because I can virtually guarantee they'll be back six months later having gained it all back and more ☹

Listen, if you leave me your phone number I PROMISE the moment I figure out how to manufacture a *"wake-up-skinny-and-stay-that-way"* pill I WILL call you, even if it's 2:00 AM and I'm sitting on the toilet with a Dostoyevsky novel and a non-alcoholic beer.

Nobody knows better than me how demoralizing it can feel to lug around all that extra weight, mine has fluctuated more than 80 pounds. And the idea of needing to lose one hundred or more pounds can be extremely overwhelming.

But instead of thinking of the hundred *(or two hundred, or 35, etc)* extra pounds you have to lose, how about telling yourself you've got just ONE pound to lose?

One hundred times. *(Adjust as needed.)*

Paradoxically, it's a LOT easier to get the ship moving in the right direction when you think this way. And remember, like Doug Graham, author of "The 80-10-10 Diet" says "Direction is MUCH more important than speed!"

THE FASTEST WAY TO LOSE WEIGHT IS SLOWLY.

SLOW WEIGHT LOSS is the ONLY solution I've ever seen people make permanent.

Of course, most of you won't listen to me about this, but what if I'm right?

One more thing!

So what if you ARE fat! I mean, I know it's unpleasant. There are health risks. It'd be better to be thinner - sure. But let's do a thought experiment to soften the way you treat yourself about this and therefore *(paradoxically)* make it more likely you'll stick to your plan and actually lose the weight.

Are you up for that? Good!

OK, now, how many of you have ever run for congress in order to introduce legislation which requires the government to gather up all people above a certain weight and put them in a special camp to keep them isolated from the thin population? If there were a referendum which suggested that all people over a certain weight *(whatever weight you find intolerable)* be executed, would you vote for it?

Or how about this, when you finally get thin, are you planning to utterly shun fat people? Will you stop being friends with anyone who happens to be carrying too much weight? Are you going to simply turn and walk away if a fat person says hello? Or asks for a hug?

Of course you wouldn't do ANY of these things. So why in the world would you EVER allow your Pig to talk to you the degrading way it does when you feel a little gravity challenged on any particular day? Can you see now how exaggerated your Pig's constant criticism of your weight is? In fact, it's only purpose is to keep you feeling too badly about yourself to be able to resist the next Binge. It wants Pig Slop, that's all it ever wants. And it's willing to sacrifice all your happiness and mental wellbeing to get it

So you're fat. So what. Big f----g deal! C'mere already and I'll give you a hug.

Trust me, fat comes off, slow and steady if you'll let it.

Oh, and do you know where it all goes? In the toilet, that's where. I bet you never thought of THAT before. *(You're welcome).*

CHAPTER 5: ENVIRONMENTAL TRIGGERS AND THEIR BUSTERS

#22 The Smell of Food

Many people report, especially in the early days of sticking to their Food Plan, that the smell of their previous binge foods is just too enticing. For example, walking by an Italian restaurant or bakery "drives them mad" and they just can't resist.

Well, first of all, please know there's nothing wrong with you if you feel this way. See, I firmly believe we overeaters don't have a disease, we have extraordinarily healthy appetites which have been corrupted by modern life. For example, we didn't have scones, pizza, and brownies in the tropics while we were evolving... these are artificial concentrations of pleasure produced by today's world (for a profit).

And realize there are many other very strong biological signals which stimulate all sorts of other cravings we must comfortably live with on a day to day basis. An attractive stranger walks into the room, you don't run up and kiss them on the lips, right? Someone cuts you off in traffic, you don't immediately ram their car, right?

As much as you may want to do these things, you've learned to live comfortably with these impulses. You don't avoid public places. You still get in your car and drive. You simply accept these things as part of the "stimuli of modern society" which you must confront most days. It's no different with food!

However, it can be very helpful to protect *new* habits in a little cocoon for a few months while they are in their infancy so they can develop strength unencumbered. And towards this end, there's a cool little trick you can use when you're trying to change yourself in this way...

Whenever you know you will be facing "irresistible" smells, walk around with a little Vicks Vapor Rub on your upper lip. The smell of the Vicks will overpower the delicious smell of the food and you won't have to contend with anywhere near the same level of aromatic stimulation.

I'd strongly recommend putting these kinds of tricks into the category of "training wheels" however. It's something you employ only the beginning as you're learning to avoid a particular temptation. In the long run, you don't want to rely on this kind of thing because it signals your Pig that the temptation is stronger than you are. In the end, you want to become the kind of person who could spend all day long in a bakery taking deep breaths without indulging because "that is not my food."

In the long run you want to cultivate confidence, not fear. But there's nothing wrong with creating a safe nursery in which your embryotic new habit can grow as it attempts to leave the womb on its own.

Vicks Vapor Rub. Who knew!?

#23 Passing Old Haunts (Restaurants, Bakeries, etc)

Never Binge Again is a unique philosophy inasmuch as it encourages you to cultivate confidence at all times rather than fear. So whereas a 12 step program would suggest you should avoid all the old places where you used to binge, I'd like to suggest it's entirely possibility to develop the ability to frequent bakeries, pizza joints, fast food restaurants, etc. if you'd like to socialize within them, no matter what your history therein.

That said, there is a period of time during the early formation of new habits and behavioral patterns of character where you might want to protect and nurture that habit in a cocoon for a few months. But after 90 days you can take off these "training wheels" and let your habit come out and face the world with confidence.

Ultimately you want to know you're the kind of person who can stand in front of any temptation without concern. Your Inner Food Demon may still lunge and thrash at any given previous binge food, like a Doberman Pincher in a very well locked cage. But ultimately a Doberman doesn't have the wherewithal to break out of that cage unless you take out the key and turn the lock.

So how do you do it?

Perhaps you might like to follow the lead from a woman I'll call Becky. See, Becky actually *owned* a bakery at the time she realized she had to stop eating flour and sugar entirely. This meant she not only had to be around it all day, she had to make it seem sexy enough to others that they'd want to buy it!

Now, you might think this was quite a dilemma, but for Becky it was simple. She was extremely successful with her "I Will Never Eat Flour or Sugar Again" rule by repeating one little mantra to herself whenever her Food Demon rattled its Cage: "That is not my food."

Yes, it really was that simple. Of course, she also kept herself well-nourished throughout the day so she'd experience less discomfort. But "That is not my food" is all she really needed.

I know it sounds crazy but you don't have to believe her, you just have to try it. Make sure your Food Rule is crystal clear so there's no ambiguity whatsoever between what is vs. isn't on your plan. Then for everything off the plan simply repeat Becky's mantra. You'll be pleasantly surprised!

#24 Lack of Planning and Preparation

There are many situations where planning and preparation can prevent low blood sugar and/or feeling as if the only possible solution is Pig Slop. Furthermore, there are some general preparatory steps you can take to *always* be ready for a difficult situation. Like keeping almonds and/or dried chick peas in your purse and/or car so you can either eat something before going out to an impromptu restaurant meeting or have something to throw in your salad. Or stopping at a fast food joint and getting a baked potato with nothing on it and a side salad without dressing. Or grilled chicken breast with no sauce. Not delicious, but enough to keep up your blood sugar. Or, guess what? They have these things called supermarkets just about everywhere now, and you're allowed to run in and out of them quickly without having to do a full weekly shopping run. Who knew!? *(I'm not recommending any particular food – just illustrating that there ARE options.)*

But in the end, occasionally you'll find yourself in a situation where you haven't eaten enough and every bone in your body says you "need" Slop in order to "survive." At these times there are several things you can tell yourself **"They won't find my bones by the refrigerator!"**

See, unless you're anorexic, the odds are pretty strong you

won't starve if you miss one meal. You'll be uncomfortable, yes. But they're probably not going to find your bones by the refrigerator with your arms desperately reaching for the handle in one last desperate attempt to survive. It takes at least a month in most cases to starve to death assuming you eat nothing at all. In many cases longer. Our species is very adept at navigating short periods where food and nutrition are not available. You'll live. It's better if you do enough planning so you don't ever have to skip a meal because it does increase the desire to binge, but missing one meal probably isn't going to kill you!

#25 Social Situations

> "Nobody can make you feel inferior without your consent" - Elanor Roosevelt, First Lady, 1933 to 1945

> "Nobody can make you overeat without your consent" - Glenn Livingston, Big Hairy Book Author 2015 - Present

OK, so here's the deal on other people getting you to overeat: Unless they tie you down to a bed, pry your jaws open, pour food in your mouth, and force you to chew and swallow, nobody can make you overeat. NOBODY!

All they can do is make you psychologically uncomfortable about eating healthy. And even this is relatively easy to overcome with practice. The trick is understanding what other people actually want from you in a group-dining situation, and virtually everyone who struggles with eating socially is doing so because they're missing the key point.

Other people do NOT want to understand why you're eating the way you are.

And the LAST thing they want to hear is ANYTHING which might imply they should consider changing their own ways around food.

What other people in a social dining situation want is for you to help them FEEL LOVED AND ACCEPTED FOR WHAT THEY WANT TO EAT, *without drawing attention to the fact this is what you're doing!*

If you're having trouble with others in a social situation, it's because you feel obligated to engage in the debate they're posing. "Just one won't hurt", "Oh c'mon, it's Saturday", "Really? I thought we all needed a little salt?"...

Don't take the bait!

There are about a dozen basic ways to do it. Ask for a doggy bag and give them a hug. Focus on the recipe. Make a joke. Say your doctor won't let you and you hate talking about it - even though it's not serious. Offer them an alternative way to love you back into their tribe "Mom, I ate a little too much at lunch, could you possibly make me some mint tea?" There are literally dozens more options once you understand the principles involved.

With a little practice you'll realize you just need to step a little to the left of the conversation and focus on their needs, not your own. Granted, it takes a little practice, but you do NOT have to consent to overeating and/or breaking your Food Plan under ANY circumstances, I promise!

#26 Nasty Comments About Your Weight

"Pffffff" snorted the in-house gym instructor, in a mix of surprise and contempt as he looked over my shoulder at the scale. I didn't really want him checking out my weight, but I couldn't figure out how to get the electric scale to work, so he came to "help."

Then he stuck around to offer his stupid opinion. But his antics didn't stop there. He turned to a friend I'd come in with and told him *(in a loud voice everyone could hear)* I should start running right away. My friend, trying to defend me, replied that we were just about to go swimming.

But the idiot continued: "Swimming won't help, he needs to run!"

And this "heartwarming" encounter happened AFTER I'd already lost 20 pounds. It's true, I still needed to lose 40 more, but I'd actually come to the gym excited and proud of my accomplishment when this living and breathing personification of the Pig took the wind out of my sails, with just a few idiotic, utterly unprofessional, and unsolicited opinions.

I won't lie...

I had a very rough few hours.

But every time that encounter came back to haunt me, I told my Pig to stuff it. I wouldn't let the Pig bring me down, even with help from outside accomplices!

Why did I tell you this story? Because YOU should treat stupid, mean or "well-intentioned" comments from others exactly the same way.

As nothing but Pig Squeals whose sole purpose is to get you to Binge! When you hear them, just tell your Pig to SHUT UP and go back to its Cage.

Then resume your life, because these Piggy thoughts are NOT worth your attention!

#27 Eating at Night

Are you good all day only to ruin your best laid health and fitness plans in the evening? Do you reward yourself with food at night? This is a VERY common problem! A lot of women I speak to describe their days in one or more of the following three ways:

- ➢ They were yelled at by their boss/a client/a co-worker through no fault of their own.
- ➢ Their workload is insane and they feel like they're always catching up and never on top of things.
- ➢ Their kids are very sweet but totally drain their energy.

And after taking so much crap during the day they feel like they've earned the right to eat 'crap' at night. Then their rules go out the window and the nightly binge commences. But don't worry, there are a few things you can do to avoid night time binges altogether...

- ➢ First, realize that reliving the stresses of the day is your Pig's way of getting you to Binge. So if you start to re-live a scene at work or at home that has you stressed, just say to your Pig "Hey, I see what you're doing here. And I'm not going to listen to your Squeals any longer, get back to your cage!"
- ➢ Second, reframe the concept of reward. See, by eating sugary and/or high-caloric crap, you are NOT rewarding yourself, you are punishing yourself. A reward would be to eat something healthy. Depending upon your particular Food Plan that might be an apple, some lettuce, or any of a number of other things with which you KNOW your body does well! Reward yourself with a healthy, vibrant, energy filled life, NOT something your body will have to recover from. As Doug Graham says "we should never have to recover from a meal!" *(It'll take some time, but if you keep at it you'll eventually feel the healthy foods ARE the reward and start looking forward to eating them, you'll no longer look at Pig Slop as a "treat" which you "deserve.")*

➢ Third, re-evaluate your self-care routines during the day. Virtually every night time eater I've worked with has eventually realized they are making too many decisions with not enough breaks during the day, and aren't adequately feeding themselves during the day either. Even an extra five minute break two or three times during the day where you get away from all input (people and things) which requires your response can make a big difference.

Finally, there's a technique that's hard to teach in written format that can help you avoid the feeling that you need a reward altogether, so you can reach nighttime feeling content and happy, and virtually eliminate this whole conflict. In fact, this technique can help you feel a LOT more content throughout the day too! I teach this technique in the 'Nighttime Eating Bonus' of the Never Binge Again Unlimited Coaching Program and Online Intensive *(www.NeverBingeAgainCoaching.com)*... and you get to keep this bonus, even if you eventually decide the program is not for you and request a full refund. You can download the 'nighttime eating bonus' right away when you reserve your spot. Click here for more information.

#28 Diet Deal Breakers

Almost every diet follows the same pattern: You start out GREAT, you eat well for a couple of days, weeks, or even months, and you feel better. You become quite proud of yourself, but then SOMETHING happens.

It could be something small like:

- An office party
- A vacation
- A particularly rough day at the office
- Someone inviting you over for dinner

Or it could be something major like

- A sickness or death in the family
- Relationship problems
- Financial problems..

So you slip and eat off of your food plan...

Then your Pig(tm) goes to town:

> ➢ "See! This diet isn't working! It works only if you're sitting at home concentrating 100% on keeping it. No one can keep this up! We need to find another one and in the meantime, we can binge, right? Yippeee!!!!" - Your Pig

Unfortunately the Pig is partly correct. You need to have the RIGHT mental tools to deal with these kinds of situations which take you OUT of your day to day routine. Without these tools you can easily slip and undo days, weeks or even months of dieting. And even simple circumstances, like being offered a cake at a party and/or arriving home late after a hard day *(when the Pig says you deserve some TLC)* can really derail you.

Fortunately the solution to all of this is relatively simple. It just requires some forethought and consideration regarding how, very specifically, you might loosen up in each of the situations.

You can think of it like the second rung of an archery target. In ordinary, every day circumstances you get up you and aim for the bullseye. In fact, you commit to it with perfection, even though you know you may forgive yourself with dignity after careful analysis if you miss it. But on these special days you aim for a very clearly defined second or third rung.

See, the key is that these special days ALSO have boundaries. You don't just run headlong into them expecting to make spontaneous good decisions, because that takes a lot of willpower, which is something decidedly hard to come by in many of these situations. You define the edges. You go in KNOWING this isn't necessarily going to be a "bullseye day" and you're OK with that because you know you ARE going to hit the second rung of the target.

What might this look like on a practical basis? The specific boundaries you draw for non-bullseye days are different for each individual, but here are some examples:

➢ One day per Calendar Week I may have one serving of desert of my choosing if I'm at someone else's home and/or out to dinner with a friend. *(With care to define what a serving is).*

➢ On Thanksgiving, Christmas, and New Year's Eve each year, if I so chose, I may eat one plateful of anything I like, but no more.

➢ I may eat 20% more calories than my normal, every day target, one day per Calendar Month at an office party.

➢ I may have one glass of wine each night at dinner while I'm on vacation.

See what I mean? The key is specificity, and ensuring that the boundaries you choose won't too seriously interfere with your health and fitness goals.

One caveat before we leave this topic: For some people with some things, NEVER is a lot easier than sometimes. See, your brain is always presenting you with a list of options when the desired behavior in a given situation isn't defined. And if SOMETIMES you eat XYZ *(usually sugar, flour, and/or alcohol),* then your brain is going to want to present XYZ as an option. For SOME people, carefully defining the limits of that option IS enough to control it without willpower. But for others, complete abstinence is the only way. *(For example, I will NEVER eat chocolate again no matter what situation life throws at me. But I DO eat dried fruit twice a week provided I have it with 8 times the volume of leafy green vegetables.)*

There IS a risk of specifying conditions under which you may indulge in a previously difficult to control substance, and that risk is yours to decide upon. Only you can know in your heart of hearts whether or not it's worth it. Often it really is. Sometimes it's really not! I wanted you to know how to take that risk if indeed you were going to.

CHAPTER 6: THOUGHT BASED TRIGGERS AND THEIR BUSTERS

#29 "One Little Bite Won't Hurt" – Start Again Tomorrow

"It's just one bite", "A little won't hurt", "C'mon, just a taste", "Only one bite or swallow", "Start your diet again tomorrow", etc.

These are perhaps the most common Squeals most people's Food Monsters™ ever make, and they're all based on ignoring several important facts:

➢ **NEUROPLASTICITY:** Research into neuroplasticity strongly suggests that you're never really standing still with your food habits. You're either reinforcing or extinguishing these neural pathways... making them stronger or weaker. Therefore, if you indulge in "one little bite today" what you've done is dig that groove in your brain just a little deeper, making it even harder to get back on track tomorrow. Plus, what's to stop you from having "one little bite" again tomorrow? On the other hand, if you don't indulge and chose to eat something healthy instead, you've both weakened the addiction to the undesirable behavior and simultaneously strengthened a healthy pathway.

➢ **TURNING THE SHIP AROUND:** Think of a massive ship making its way from New York to London across the Atlantic. Now suppose the Captain notices a Twinkie drifting by and the boat just missed it. So he decides to turn the whole ship around to go get it.

That takes a lot more fuel than you might think because in order to do so he has to fight the momentum which was previously headed in the right direction. All that energy goes into stopping the ships forward momentum and then actually accelerating in the wrong direction. Then, once the Twinkie is retrieved, even more fuel is required to stop the backward momentum, turn the ship around yet again, and accelerate once more in the right direction.

But it's not just the fuel costs. Consider the delay imposed by maneuvering the ship in this kind of impulsive manner. Because of the dual directional shift, it may be several hours before the ship is even back in the same location it started in when it noticed the Twinkie.

Plus, the kind of captain who jumps after Twinkies in this way is unlikely to stop at just one. He'll likely go after all sorts of other stuff in the ocean as his impulses may dictate when he sees the opportunity. And you know, when it comes to binge eating, there's almost never such a thing as "just one bite" ... so those hours are measured in days, weeks, months, and sometimes even years.

I once knew of a guy who lost 500 pounds by eliminating frankfurters. Then his Food Monster talked him into "just one bite of a hot dog" at a ballgame. He gained all the weight back and more. Must've been a big frankfurter!

➢ **NOW IS ALL THERE IS:** You get the point. Every bite counts. Every last one. The only time you can stop overeating is now. So always use the present moment to be healthy!

And if you're in a hole, stop digging!

One little bite off your Food Plan always hurts. It kills your confidence and your feeling of integrity. Give your Pig an inch and it will take a mile. *One bite off your Food Plan is a tragedy.* That doesn't mean all is lost and you should just let your Pig "go to town" for a while if you make a mistake. If you do make a mistake, take it seriously. Analyze what went wrong and make adjustments to your aim if need be, then forgive yourself with dignity and aim at the target again. Nevertheless, one bite off your plan IS a tragedy.

#30 This is Your "Last Chance" - Tomorrow You'll Start Being Good Forever

Look, you absolutely CAN make a plan and stick to it indefinitely, so it's entirely possible you'll never again eat the Slop you've chosen to eliminate from your diet…

But this is definitely NOT your last chance!

I'd be willing to bet my left testicle *(and I'm rather fond of that one)* there's not going to be a government decree which makes it illegal for industry to keep manufacturing the bags, boxes, and containers which are slowly killing you, or for the myriad of restaurants in your area to keep piling added sugar, salt, starch, and fat into the delicious dishes your Pig loves.

And I'd bet the right one that supermarkets aren't going to stop selling crap any time soon. They still sell cigarettes for goodness' sake!!

Short of a nuclear war—and probably not even then—I think you can rest confident in the fact there will be Pig Slop. There always has been and there always will be. So tell your Pig to be quiet about this "last chance" B.S. OK?

#31 When the Scale Doesn't Budge Despite Doing Everything Right

The scale is probably the source of more trouble for overeaters than anything else. But used right, it can also be your best friend. It's an objective measure. Yes, it's quite flawed in the short run due to wild fluctuations associated with salt, time of the month, volume of food eaten, exercise, dehydration/hydration, timing of your bowel movements, etc. But over time, with dozens *(or ideally hundreds)* of weigh-ins the noise falls out and the trend becomes clear.

One of the WORST Squeals about the scale is "You're doing everything right and you haven't lost an ounce! It's not worth it, let's just binge and be done with trying!"

The Pig insists if the scale does not move quickly downwards your efforts count for nothing and you might as well binge. But it can take some significant time for your body to realize it's no longer living in a feast and famine environment so it's safe to start letting go of the weight. Because if you're like most overeaters, you're probably not just good at overdoing food, you're good at *underdoing* it too!

Regular, reliable nutrition and calories will signal your body it doesn't need to hold onto extra fat for upcoming times of scarcity. Give it time! The fastest way to lose weight is *slowly* because if you drop pounds too quickly your body will fight back. It will eventually insist you hoard calories and nutrition the moment it sees they are once again abundantly available, which, in our society, is always just around the corner.

Secondly, not GAINING weight counts for something, doesn't it!? Most people caught up in binge eating will attest to the fact pounds come on much faster than they'd ever imagined. So just stopping the ship from moving in the wrong direction is a big accomplishment. Celebrate!

Last, recall when, exactly, your last binge was. How much damage did it do? *If you had eliminated that binge, where might your weight be now?* The Pig wants you to forget the damage done by binging and assign blame for the weight stagnancy to your Food Plan so it can get you to say "screw it – it's no use, might as well keep binging." But upon reflection and careful analysis, most often I find it is the binging that's causing the weight stagnancy, not the Food Plan! *(If people would just stay with what they're doing long enough to give it a chance without a binge they might find nothing needs changing!)*

#32 I Just Binged Therefore I Must Binge Again

"I Binged After Five Clean Weeks and I'm Devastated"

I hear something of this sort from clients with frequency. "I Caged the Pig for 5 WEEKS, but yesterday it came out. I'm devastated, I don't know what to do. I'm SO overwhelmed and frightened." :-(

Well, first off, being binge free for five weeks is an AMAZING accomplishment.

That's 840 hours without binging compared to just 1 hour of overeating. It's critically important to note this because your Pig would prefer you to focus all your attention on that solitary hour. It WANTS you to feel devastated and overwhelmed, because that makes it much more likely you'll feel too weak to resist letting it out to Binge again.

But it turns out if you focus on the 840 hours of success instead, your Pig hardly stands a chance!

Also, after a Binge your Pig will say says it's "totally unhinged" and insist it will take a serious effort to get it bound again. Of course, in the meantime, it says you might as well just Binge.

Poor Pig.

It doesn't realize you do NOT need a Herculean effort - because what worked in the past will most likely work in the future!...

JUST PUT THE PIG BACK...as in one nanosecond after the LAST bite of Slop you fed it.

Then figure out what went wrong which made that first bite of Slop possible, and, if necessary, adjust your Food Plan to prevent that in the future. *(Or dispute the Squeal which tricked you into breaking the Food Rule).*

And that's it.

Bingeing once CAN be a disaster which unravels you, but ONLY if you allow your Pig to make it into one. Otherwise...it's just a learning experience, no matter how bad it was.

Here's another perspective to help you overcome the guilt and shame so you can forgive yourself and move on after a Binge. You can reverse the shame and guilt by becoming a better parent to yourself. Let me explain...

Imagine you have a child with an eating problem and she's trying her absolute best to solve it. Then, one day, she comes to you crying and confesses a Binge.

At that juncture you COULD decide to be a strict, cruel parent. You could yell at her, call her a worthless child, say she'll always be fat... that she'll NEVER learn how to eat well and it's hopeless to even try. You could tell her to just continue binging because she's such a disgrace to your family.

OR... you could be a kind parent. You could tell her you love her very much despite the binge. You could give her a hug, sit down with her, and try to figure out why she binged and how she can avoid it in the future. Then you could hug her again and tell her you're 100% confident in her and tell her once again that you love her no matter what.

Which parent would you chose to be? The kind one ...right? In your mind, isn't that strict parent a horrible person? You'd NEVER consciously and purposefully allow yourself to become anything like her, right? Yet after we binge, we all behave like that cruel parent TO OURSELVES.

Unfortunately, because you've spent years being the cruel parent when it comes to your own eating, it can be difficult to just stop on a dime. But you CAN begin to include the kind parent in your inner dialog. So when the 'cruel' inner voice starts to torment you, push it aside as if it were the cruel parent. Say "there's no place for you here!" and then ask yourself what the kindest parent in the world would say in her stead.

#33 Can't Decide Which Diet to Follow

Do you ever feel confused about which diet to follow? One day it's low carb or paleo, the next high carb, macrobiotics, or one of those calorie-counting or points systems? Does it ever seem like if you could just stop jumping from diet to diet you might be fine... you just don't know which one to choose because they all seem right AND they all seem wrong?

If so, you may be suffering from your Pig's attempts to confuse and conquer you with something I call "The Grass is Greener on the Other Side" syndrome.

See, in a state of uncertainty your Pig prevails. If it's not clear what the rules are then, the Pig reasons, anything goes. That's the motivation behind keeping you in a constantly confused state about what diet and/or Food Plan to follow. It does this with "trash talk" in much the same way boxers psych out their opponents...

See, the very best Boxers have a unique ability...they REALLY know how to "trash talk!" They'll use TV interviews, social media and really every opportunity they have to tell their would be opponent how weak he is, how they're going to break him, leave him bloodied on the boxing-ring floor...how they'll humiliate him in front of his family and friends...how he's worthless, stupid loser who doesn't stand a chance of winning...

They do this all the way up to the fight...even inside the ring they KEEP trash talking...because when trash talk succeeds it gets the other guy to forget his plan, to forget the technique he spent years perfecting, to act out of fear and anger...

Which is exactly when they calmly step up that poor other guy and knock him out.

Well, I've got news for you...your Pig is doing the very same thing to get you to jump from diet to diet. It says something like...

> ➢ "Hey... we've tried this diet for a whole week (or month, etc.) now and not only haven't we lost any weight, we actually gained a little...and we even had to cheat a bunch because obviously this is NOT the diet for us... so let's just try the next one. In the meantime, we can have us a big hairy Binge, can't we? Pretty please!!?" – Your Pig

The solution to this dilemma is to pick ONE diet that's anywhere close to reasonable and stick to it, even if it's not perfect. See, when it comes to binge eating, people do MUCH better when they have a clear target to aim for. It's just too tempting to eat anything and everything when you don't. If the diet turns out to be less than perfect, you can modify it later. Consult a dietitian, doctor, or nutritionist for help. Just don't allow a state of uncertainty to prevail because that's a losing game.

The grass isn't greener on the other side, the grass is greener where it's watered!

If you FOCUS on a reasonable Food Plan, no matter how imperfect, you will learn how to implement it better and better. If you jump from plan to plan, you'll NEVER get the requisite experience...you'll always be a Food Plan Rookie! Don't be a Food Plan Rookie...pick a plan and water it! You can fix it later.

#34 Worrying You'll Be Tortured with Deprivation Forever

Sometimes when you consider letting go of and/or regulating some toxic-but-pleasurable substance in your life *(e.g. sugar, flour, alcohol, caffeine, etc)* your Pig will jump in and say "Oh no! You simply can't do that! I will torture you with cravings forever (and ever!)"

BUT YOU WILL NOT HAVE TORTUROUS CRAVINGS FOREVER.

See, every choice we make either helps reinforce or extinguish our addictions. And this is why the Pig Squeals so loudly when you begin to seriously consider letting go. It knows if you ignore its Squeal, its energy for Squealing is going to be less the next time. And the time after that. And the time after that...

But if you feed the Pig's Squeal its energy will increase, and you will be tortured by even more cravings. It's a simple formula really - "that which fires together wires together" *(neuroplasticity in the scientific literature)* ...

Feed a craving and it gets stronger.

Starve it and it gets weaker...

Until within a few months it's virtually non-existent.

Moreover, when you have less hyper-addictive, supersized stimuli in your diet *(we didn't have chocolate bars, potato chips, pretzels, candy, cake, etc. in the tropics while we were evolving– these are artificially concentrated forms of pleasure that evolution has not prepared us for),* your taste buds and neurological pleasure systems begin to respond more forcefully to what nature has to offer. Stop eating a chocolate bar every day and before you know it an apple tastes sweet again. Stay stopped long enough and you'll very much enjoy the subtle differences between different species of apples – e.g. Gala vs. Envy vs. Delicious vs. Fuji, etc.

Before long you will hardly crave chocolate at all, despite your Pig's protests.

I know I mentioned this earlier, but I want to go into more detail here.

See, I haven't eaten chocolate in years, and I can't remember the last time my Pig Squealed for it. I literally walk by the smells, sites, and sounds of chocolate in the supermarket and think NOTHING of it. I don't even have to remember why I don't eat it anymore. I don't have to remember all the best answers to the Pig's crazy rationalizations for eating it...

Because chocolate does NOT look like a treat to me anymore! To me it seems like some chemicals in a brown wrapper. Might as well be poop. I'm not eating it either way.

But when I first thought about giving up chocolate my Pig(tm) was louder than I'd ever heard it. I thought it was impossible. I thought I'd be driven crazy forever with Cravings. But I decided chocolate was Pig Slop(tm) and I would never eat it again... so I didn't... and those Cravings went away a LOT sooner than I expected.

Unfortunately, I know from experience with other things on

my Never list *(and from working with so many clients)* that even one bite would bring back the memories and the Cravings again...but since I Will Never Eat Chocolate Again, I don't have to worry about that at all. My Plan is to FORGET chocolate entirely, even though my Pig would like me to remember. And for all intents and purposes I HAVE forgotten it...

And that, my friends, is bliss.

You don't have to give up chocolate if you don't have a problem with it... this was just for illustration. But if your Pig is telling you you're going to be tortured forever related to any of its Slop, just tell it to STF up because you know those are just the desperate few last Squeals of a condemned prisoner.

Food for thought!

#35 "This Can't Work Forever – Sooner or Later You'll Binge" – Sincerely, Your Pig

Most overeaters are bothered by their history. Their Pig is all too fond of telling them "Listen, go ahead and try any diet you want to. You've done it a thousand times before and you've always failed. Therefore, it's only a matter of time until you do again. I've really got you now, don't I smarty-pants!? Yippeee!!"

There are a multitude of flaws with this line of thinking.

First of all, people change, and those who lose weight and keep it off permanently usually have many more attempts behind them than people who stay heavy. Getting up and trying again is the hallmark of people who win this game. So, your Pig is actually complimenting your resilience and persistence when it points out you're trying yet again!

Second, if nobody could ever change course then nothing would ever get done in our society, ever. Progress always comes from taking a different road. And driving 1,000 miles on a highway without taking an exit says nothing about your ability to take the very next one. You can get off an undesirable highway taking you in the wrong direction any time you want. And any stock market analyst will tell you "past history is not a good indicator of future performance." It's the de-facto disclaimer.

Third, everyone can think of something in their life which they couldn't accomplish for a long time, but which they eventually did through persistence, guidance, and fortitude. Some subject at school they struggled with for a while. Learning to dance. How to cook. Even how to walk. Pretty much EVERYTHING worthwhile in life takes a multitude of attempts. Sometimes years. And your willingness to get up and keep trying is the definition of success!

But most importantly, the ONLY time you can stop overeating is now. Right this very moment. You can't do anything about what you put in your mouth five years, five months, five days, or even five minutes ago, but you CAN use the present moment to be healthy.

Similarly, unless you've got a blueprint for a time machine with enough money and connections to obtain a quantum flux capacitor, dilithium crystal, and a near-light-speed accelerator, you're NOT going to be able to warp into the future and convince yourself to stop then...but at this very moment, NOW, you have control over your legs, arms, mouth, and tongue, and you are entirely capable of deciding exactly what does and doesn't go into your mouth. Only YOU will decide what to chew, swallow, and digest.

You CAN (and must) always use the present moment to be healthy. In fact, it's the ONLY moment you'll ever control. Because even as I write this, it is ALWAYS now. My last sentence *("because even as I write this...")* is already in the past. And

NOW the last one *("my last sentence...")* has faded into the past too. But I have full control over everything I am writing as these words fall onto the page, and I can choose exactly what to say...

Just as YOU can choose exactly what to eat NOW.

We always must use the present moment to be healthy. Now is the ONLY moment of choice. And to paraphrase Sartre', we can choose to remake ourselves at any moment.

What are YOU doing right now?

Food for thought!

#36 Not Enough Time for Self Care

I find most people who struggle keeping their own food commitments have NO trouble keeping their commitments to other people. They often have very regular routines for taking care of their spouses, children, grandchildren. Many have VERY stressful jobs with ongoing commitments, deadlines, and bosses to please. Some are avidly involved with volunteer work at their church, temple, or mosque, and still others have hobby-based commitments to friends and family which take up a good deal of their time.

What all these people seem to have in common is the virtually flawless execution of their commitments to other people...they always put OTHERS first! But that's unfortunately the WRONG mindset for sticking with your own diet! You've got to put yourself first...

And NO! This is NOT selfish! Because you'll actually be BETTER at taking care of others if you do. Think of it like this: The standard advice for getting through an emergency loss of oxygen and/ or air pressure in an airplane is to be sure you've secured YOUR OWN mask before taking care of your children or the people next to you, because you're NO GOOD to them if you can't breathe yourself.

Healthy food is like oxygen...it energizes and breathes life into you so you CAN take care of those around you. But junk food is like carbon dioxide... it drains the life from you and makes you of MUCH less value to those around you. Make no mistake about it, your Pig wants you to mix this up...it wants you to put everyone else's needs before your own...so you'll take care of them and feel too weak and drained to resist its call to overeat...but now you know better.

Put on your own oxygen mask first, whatever that means in your own healthy self-care and eating routine, whether that means making the time to go shopping, doing food prep, calling ahead to the restaurant to be sure you'll have something to eat, taking the time to meditate, exercise, take a nap, or do whatever else YOU need to do to be sure YOU are well, energized, and ready for life...

Because the alternative does NOBODY any good!

#37 You Will Have to Remain Vigilant Forever (and Forever is Way Too Long)

This is really a variation on the "This Can't Work Forever" Squeal, but people often ask if they'll need to be constantly vigilant to be sure their Pig doesn't fool them. If it will require a lifetime of effort to control it and ensure they eat well. The answer is a definitive...

NO!

See, your Pig is really just a bodily organ you're getting control over and redirecting towards healthier aims and goals. It's not unlike your ovaries, testes, and/or bladder. All these bodily organs generate powerful biological urges and will continue to do so for life. Yet through a simple process of socialization and character commitment, we can all learn not to pee in public and/or grab attractive people and kiss them just because our bodily organs generate a powerful drive to do so.

You can't excise the Reptilian Brain from your body any more than you could remove your bladder. But you can build and reinforce the neurological pathways which direct its drives towards aims that YOU consciously and purposefully choose when you're of sound mind and body and able to exercise your intellect. You can also extinguish the destructive pathways which connect those drives to Pig Slop. *(Every craving is an opportunity to deny the Pig, feed the AUTHENTIC need, and thereby make the addictive pathway weaker!)*

Another analogy might be learning how to drive. You have to learn how to manage a LOT of impulses based upon a set of rules *(the rules of the road)* before you get a license. But shortly thereafter everything kind of settles down and becomes rote. You don't have to think about it.

Also - if you stick with it long enough, and you DO pay attention to nourishing your body on a regular and sustained basis, the cravings die to almost nothing.

I hope that helps.

#38 I Can't Afford to Enjoy Eating Healthy – The Persimmon Paradox

Persimmons are far and away my favorite food. They outrank everything including chocolate, pasta, pizza, bread and butter, bagels, black and white cookies, onion soup, salmon, fried clams, applesauce… even my mother's tuna casserole. *(Sorry Mom!)* In fact, as they're only available for about 6 weeks in the fall each year, if you happen across a ripe one in February, I might be willing to sell you certain non-vital organs for a bite.

But I had a strange experience at Whole Foods *(our organic grocery)* on the first week they were available this fall. I go shopping most Sundays. And I practically fainted when I walked into the store and saw a display full of hundreds of them. HEAVEN, I thought!

I rushed to the display and started filling up a gigantic bag with about 14 of them. *(You can't eat'm before they're ripe by the way or you're going to throw up – seriously!)*

Then... I paused.

Because the season just started, and they were $1.49 EACH.

Which meant I was going to be shelling out about $20 for the bag.

And despite what I just told you *(I'd almost sell you my Mom for a bag)*, despite the fact that $20 isn't very much money to me these days...

A big hairy price policeman in my head shouted "NO WAY GLENN... YOU CAN'T PAY $20 FOR A BAG OF FRUIT!!!"

And therein lies the problem.

How much money had I spent on binge food over the years? How much was the TIME worth that I lost in productivity due to having to recover from Pig Slop? I can't even begin to estimate, but I can tell you it's at least hundreds of times more than $20.

But there's good news.

I did indeed buy the big bag of persimmons and walked out with my head held high.

Do you know why?

Because I remembered how I used to spend $40 on "Decaf Venti Soy Lattes with No Foam" at Starbucks each and every week.

And I said to myself "I'll be damned if I'm going to let Starbucks hijack my brain into believing I should spend twice the money on a quarter of the nutrition and a tenth of the pleasure of this big bag of organic fruit in front of me!"

AT THAT MOMENT I'D BROKEN THE PIG'S PRICING SPELL.

Why in the world couldn't I INVEST IN MYSELF for something which was COMPLETELY within my Food Rules, totally healthy for me in my own dietary philosophy, and probably the taste I enjoy most in this life!?

I castrated the Pig's Pricing Squeal.

Makes sense?

Yah, it does!

#39 Autopilot "Unconscious" Binges

A Simple Strategy to Deal with Autopilot Eating:

MANY of my clients say their binges do not begin with a "Pig Squeal." They insist they hear NOTHING prior to the overeating episode. Heck, some of them even describe a strange, almost out-of-body experience where they suddenly find themselves in the kitchen, overeating.

Here's how you deal with this: Begin by writing down EVERYTHING you did prior to your last binge. Take your time and try to provide as many details as possible. What did you do the morning of the binge? What happened during the day? What were you doing, specifically, in the hour prior to the binge? Again, make sure to describe things with as much detail as possible. Don't just write "I was watching TV", instead write "I was watching the Oscars and was happy as a clam when Frances McFamousLady won!"

Then describe what you ate during the binge, if possible, in what order, and exactly where you were while you ate it. What did it look like before you had the first bite? Smell like? Did you have any second thoughts? *(Think carefully – you were there!)*

Now...

Two things will happen when you do this exercise. The first is that you'll be amazed by the amount of details you can recall. You'll realize you were NOT in a "Pig Induced Haze" after all. You can remember almost everything. And the thing is, you'll realize you COULD have intervened at any point to stop the binge. Every single memory along the path was an opportunity to take back control. You DECIDED not to do this. You weren't "unconscious", you had a Conscious Pig Party.

This is much better than giving away your power, because if you can decide to let the Pig out you can also decide to put it back in. If, on the other hand, you let the Pig convince you that you are powerless whenever it wants to knock you out and take over, then you'll walk around feeling terrified of the next time this "mysterious force" is going to take control. Better to feel just a little guilt for having decided than forever feel at the mercy of your Pig.

The second thing you'll discover is that some emotion or event triggered a 'squeal' that 'justified' the binge. For example, one of our clients discovered she "auto binges" every time she talks to her mother on the phone. Another client discovered she binged on particularly stressful days at work. We eliminated both problems by constructing simple rules around those squeals. For example "I always eat a big salad after I talk to my mother in the evening." Or "I never leave the house for work without packing lunch for myself first.")

Don't buy the Pig's false claims to power.

#40 We've Been Really Good for a While

How to Celebrate a Few Binge Free Days: Here's a sneaky Pig Squeal most of my clients have succumbed to at one point or another...

> ➢ "Hey, we've been REALLY good for a few days. Let's celebrate by having ourselves a great big yummy Binge!" Sincerely, Your Pig

But Pig Slop is NOT a celebration. It will only take you out of the present moment and give you something to recover from and feel badly about, most often on a very profound level. The way to celebrate a few binge free days is with a few MORE binge free days! You gave yourself a present, now give yourself another one, ad infinitum!

#41 These Cravings Will Last FOREVER If You Don't Give In

I've got GREAT news! Your cravings will NOT last forever, even though your Pig says you'll be indefinitely tortured by them. Let me explain.

See, if you sleep under a subway like I did in graduate school, it only takes a few weeks before you don't really hear it anymore. Your nervous system "down-regulates" its response to this SUPER-SIZED stimulus. *(The subway noises.) Similarly*, if you eat a chocolate bar every day your body will down-regulate its response to the natural sugars in fruit and vegetables. They just won't taste sweet any more.

In fact, this can get so bad that some people feel they need the candy just to "feel normal."

But the opposite is also true. Move away from the subway and you'll start to be more sensitive to loud noises again within a matter of weeks. Stop eating sugar and your taste buds should regenerate and double in sensitivity in the same time frame.

Your Pig says you'll be tortured forever without its favorite junk, but it's LYING, I promise! You already know how I extinguished my chocolate cravings. But did you know the very same thing happened to me with flour? It took about 8 weeks for 80% of the cravings to go away, then at the six months mark I'd say they were 80% diminished again *(maybe 5% of what they once were).*

Last thing - the extinction curve *(wherein the cravings diminish roughly according to the schedule I described - in my experience)* gets reset every time you let the Pig out. And resets at a lower level if you're managing these things conditionally...

Sorry - I didn't make the rules – so please don't shoot the messenger! ☹ But that's why it's so important to remember at every moment that we are either reinforcing or extinguishing our addictions. There really is no in-between.

Oh, one more thing while we're on the topic. While you DO have cravings, please remember they activate your fight or flight response in the sympathetic nervous system. Your body thinks it's an "emergency." It follows that you can calm them down somewhat with anything that activates the *parasympathetic* nervous system instead. Tense all your muscles while you take a deep breath, then let them all go when you breathe out. Do some meditation. Go for a walk. Pet your dog. Hug your kids. Anything that calms the body down and takes it out of survival mode should help with the urge to binge too.

#42 I Really Need to Make Up for My Binge by Fasting or Strict Dieting

Hey, there's something VERY IMPORTANT about food addiction most people don't realize: Overeating is an addiction to a TWO-SIDED CYCLE that fools your survival drive, constantly keeps you in "fight or flight" mode, and creates a vicious downward spiral.

Essentially what happens is after each binge most people try to make up for it by going through a period of fasting, juicing, exercising, or dieting. And in so doing they create some type of serious caloric and/or nutritional deficiency.

In other words, after each FEAST they put their body through a FAMINE, and what they don't realize is that BOTH the feast and the famine parts of this cycle are addicting because both signal your brain that calories and nutrition are only available during certain brief periods of time.

Both sides of the feast and famine coin keep you in a kind of "fight or flight" survival mode, where your sympathetic nervous system is all ramped up so you're alert for a possible "emergency" that might require action. *(Mostly that action is finding an emergency source of high calories and nutrition. But unfortunately this drive is then hijacked by industrial food-like-substances which fool but never satisfy it.)*

Bulimia, by the way, makes this all about 10x worse by creating an ACTUAL emergency in the body.

That's why it's SO important to understand that the solution to binge eating, in my not so humble opinion, is always to signal your brain there's a regular and reliable source of nutrition and calories available. As my colleague Wendy Hendry, author of the bestselling book “W.A.I.T. Loss” says "You've got to eat breakfast after a binge, even if you don't want to!"

#43 Forgetting Your Food Rules

What If You "Forget" Your Food Rules?

It's funny, there are so many other commitments in life where we don't allow ourselves the excuse of forgetting... but when it comes to food, we're not only sure it's going to happen, we're so frightened of it we decide to put off the decision to change almost indefinitely. "What if I forget?" people commonly say. Well, if this Squeal troubles you, here's how you can put it to rest:

First, consider other commitments where forgetting just isn't an option. You can't use "I won't sleep with anyone else unless I forget" as a vow at your wedding. You can't tell a policeman you simply forgot the speed limit. You can't tell the bank you simply forgot you had a mortgage to pay. Remembering is part of partaking of adult responsibilities, privileges, and freedoms in our society.

Second, you can think of EVERY food rule you create as being preceded by the words "consciously and purposefully." So "I will never eat chocolate Monday through Friday again" becomes "I will never consciously and purposefully eat chocolate Monday through Friday again." That way, if you DO actually forget, you won't have broken your rules, but the moment you realize what's happened you'll be obligated to get back on plan.

See, what the Pig is up to in the "what if I forget" game is getting you to put off the decision to stop dilly-dallying with Slop and get on with your health and fitness goals. But we're on to its game, aren't we.

Game, set, and match!

Put an END to the uncertainty about your ability to remain on your plan forever!

#44 What If You Don't Believe You Can Cage Your

Pig?

If you really don't believe you can cage your Pig you'll want to try *this* one simple thing…

See, I'll let you in on a little secret...

There's only ONE thing holding most people back when it comes to caging their Pig...

It's THE thing preventing them from getting to their goal weight, from getting the figure they want... in fact... it's the one thing that's holding them back from getting the entire LIFE they crave...

That one thing is ... CONFIDENCE!

Let's be honest, it's just the two of us here, right? If you are reading this, there's a good chance you have at least some doubts that you can cage your Pig, at least not for long. But there's one thing you can do to get confidence quickly...

Intentionally put yourself through a very tough situation.

For example, go to your favorite Pig Slop joint, order a bottle of water (only), and sit there for 30 minutes and watch OTHER people eat the Slop your Pig believes it can't live without...*then walk out without eating a single bite.* And then go another 24 hours without binging...whatever it takes!

Don't try to lose weight during this experiment, in fact, you should eat PLENTY of healthy food before, during, and after this confidence rocket. The point of this exercise is not to lose weight, it's to demonstrate to yourself that you are MUCH tougher than you thought. Infinitely tougher than your Pig as a matter of fact.

And the next time the Pig screams for Slop, recall this win, remember how strong you were, and tell it to STF up because NOTHING will prevent you from pursuing the life you want.

Got it? Good! Go for it!

#45 What If Never Binge Again Doesn't Work for ME?

WHAT IF NEVER BINGE AGAIN DOESN'T WORK FOR YOU?

This may seem like an odd thing for me to say, but there's nothing to "work" or "not work" in the Never Binge Again system! That's because NBA is only a codification of common sense tied up in a neat little package which (a) makes it clear we've all got free will and the ability to control ourselves; (b) helps us to define our trouble spots and decide how we wish to deal with them going forward.

Never Binge Again is NOT like an operation, pill, or medication which works ON you. It can't MAKE you eat healthy. It just eliminates all the prairie pooh out there which suggests we can't control ourselves and argues against trying in any sort of meaningful way. That's right, NBA is NOT a treatment. It's just well organized, very palatable, easily implemented information about RESTORING YOUR ABILITY TO CHOOSE. But when one restores the ability to CHOOSE, one also gets the ability to CHOOSE NOT TO.

Now, I'd argue it's infinitely healthier to know you're CHOOSING not to eat healthy than to believe you're at the mercy of a mysterious disease and/or overwhelming irresistible force. Because at least when you recognize the choice, you can do something about it next time, as opposed to sliding further and further down the abyss while you wait for something to "work for" you.

NOTHING WILL EVER WORK <u>FOR</u> YOU...EXCEPT YOU!

You DO have a choice no matter what your Pig says about food, no matter what it's done in the past, nor how many times it has done it! Which choice will YOU make?

CHAPTER 7: MOTIVATIONAL THOUGHTS, TIPS, AND TRICKS TO GET YOU THROUGH THE IMPULSE TO BINGE

"The painful burden of not having tried is heavier than your personal barbell will ever be"

Unknown Author

This last section may be the most powerful and is intended to multiply the effectiveness of everything discussed in the 45 Triggers section above. Contained herein you'll find motivational insights which don't neatly fit with any given trigger, yet can be applied to virtually ANY of them. Don't skip this – you'll thank me, I promise.

The Ultimate Solution to Your Food Problem in

Three Words

Want to know the essence of your food problem in one sentence? Your Pig wants you to start eating healthy "later," but the ONLY time you can actually eat healthy is right this very moment! If you indulge today, the impulse to indulge tomorrow will be stronger, which means when tomorrow comes, "later" will be even *more* appealing. That's just how our neurology works. So your ONLY real option is to:

EAT HEALTHY NOW!

NOW AS IN RIGHT THIS VERY MINUTE! Not "right after you finish that cupcake, bag of chips, donut, etc" - right fricking now! You must always use the present moment to be healthy. Always. So if there's something in your hands or your mouth which shouldn't be there as you read this, get up from chair and/or put down your smartphone, walk over to the garbage and throw the rest of the damn thing out! And if you're in the middle of chewing and swallowing something you know is poisonous to you personally, go to the bathroom and spit it out in the toilet where it belongs. No matter how much you had already you'll be better off without those extra bites. It'll be the first strong signal to yourself of your commitment to eat healthy now and always.

Oh, and since it's ALWAYS now, if you live by this mantra over and over again ("eat healthy now") then you'll ALWAYS eat healthy FOREVER. You can live out the balance of your life without the dark cloud of "later" hanging over your head. It really is that simple!

Use Evidence of Success to Win the Food Battle

I've mentioned many times how the Pig discourages us by focusing on evidence of FAILURE. If you slip up just once, your Pig will use this single, solitary mistake to try and prove you can't change and nothing you can ever do will help you stop overeating. But you do NOT have to use the Pig's 'evidence of failure' lens. You can choose to collect 'evidence of success' instead and create a positive feedback loop to provide the energy and motivation you'll need to tighten up your food plan and stick to it until it becomes second nature.

How do you collect evidence of success? Start by answering the questions below about your relationship with food since you've read Never Binge Again:

- Have you been able to avoid binging even once when you might not have before? Perhaps on a number of occasions?

- Did you stop gaining weight, even if you haven't lost any? Or perhaps you just slowed down the rate at which you were gaining?

- Have you lost a single pound? Perhaps a few?

- Were you able to reject some previously irresistible food offered to you *(at least once)?*

- Did you avoid overeating at least once at a social event where you would've had trouble before?

- Have you clearly defined even ONE food rule? Perhaps a few?

- Were you able to attribute the excess shame and guilt associated with mistakes at least once to the Pig? *(It wants you to focus on the shame and guilt so you'll feel too weak to resist the NEXT binge)* More than once?

If you've answered YES to ONE question, then you've already started your transformation...

If you've answered YES to THREE questions then you are well on your way to totally changing your relationship with food.

And if you've answered YES to FOUR or more questions then you are doing extremely well and should be very encouraged!

See what we did there? We did NOT focus on what you **didn't** do, we focused on what you **did** do successfully. Do that daily and you'll be golden!

Finding Meaning, Purpose and Significance in Never Binge Eating Again

The ability to stick to a commitment is the ability to step out of the jungle and recognize what makes us human. To forgo short term gratification for a longer-term goal is the essence of what makes civilization possible.

To master your bodily impulses and place them firmly under the control of your higher brain functions is what drives self-actualization.

To say "I Will Never Binge Again" is really to say "I am not merely an animal - I am a human being - capable of contribution beyond measure, and as such I will make all my difficult food choices with my intellect rather than my emotions."

Your Inner Pig hates this. It does not want you to find your true self. It does not want you to feel a sense of mastery and capability in the world. It prefers that you endlessly obsess about being inadequate and incapable. That your life has no meaning and the only thing of value is Pig Slop.

But the truth is you are valuable beyond measure. In the absence of Slop, we are all capable of amazing, soul inspiring things. It's a birthright!

To say "I Will Never Eat Pig Slop Again" is an obvious and crude simplification of what is, at its core, a declaration of character, meaning, and purpose. What it really means is "I am a human being and I refuse to be at the mercy of my animalistic impulses. I now recognize I can, must, and will take conscious control of directing them towards constructive human goals. From this day forward I declare myself superior to these impulses and fully capable of channeling them into meaningful and purposeful endeavors rather than wasting them on meaningless short-term pleasures and recovery from same.

I am powerful, strong, and capable beyond measure. From this day forward my impulses will serve ME - I refuse to continue as a slave to them.

I Will Never Binge Again!

Say "I Don't" NOT "I Can't"

There's a WORLD of difference between "I can't eat _____" and "I don't eat ______" but most people never give it a second thought! See, when you say, "I can't eat sugar", for example, you've assumed a childlike mentality. Some big bad grown up-out there, maybe your doctor, maybe your spouse, says you can't have it. This makes you feel deprived, angry, and eager to rebel. On the other hand if you say "I don't eat sugar" you are indicating you've made a conscious and purposeful, adult choice. You've weighed the pros and cons, assessed the benefits, and made the best decision you could at a time when you were of sound mind and body. A decision of character, to become the kind of person who doesn't eat sugar.

So to eat healthy and stick to your commitments, make it a

practice to say "I don't", NOT "I can't".

Does this make sense or does this make sense?

Don't Ask "Why Can't I ___?" Ask "How Can I ____?" Instead!

This one tip is really simple, but exceptionally important!

When you ask "Why can't I stop overeating?" what you're actually doing is asking your brain to go find evidence that you can't stop eating. And if you collect enough evidence that you can't do it, guess what, you're going to believe you can't and develop a failure identity ☹

On the other hand, if you ask "How can I stop overeating?" you'll be programming your brain to go out and find all the evidence it can to convince you that you CAN stop overeating. You'll develop a success identity, and you'll see that you CAN do it.

Don't ask "Why Can't I?" ask "How Can I?" instead.

You might want to get a tattoo to remind you. *(Legal – it's totally up to you if you want to get a tattoo or not. You can be just as successful without one. But hey, you might want to. Please don't blame your mid-life crisis on this book if you do. But if you DO get one, please send me a picture OK? support@neverbingeagain.com. But just pictures please. No showing up at my house. Unless you happen to be an intelligent, attractive, health-obsessed, affectionate, empathic, marriage minded beauty with a thing for middle aged Jewish doctors, exercise, old movies, and warm climates. There, I think that's clear now.)*

Do You Ever Feel Lost?

Here's another perspective on the above.

Do you ever feel lost? I mean REALLY lost? Like not even the spark of the man or woman you once were, with all those hopes, dreams, and determination to change the world that comes with youth, is anywhere to be found?

Are the embers of those once beautiful flames buried SO deep under the pile of bad food (or other addictions) you've put through your body that you worry the fire can't ever be rekindled?

That you won't ever find the mindset you need to stop doing all those negative things and move on with the balance of your life?

Are you waiting to rekindle your fire before you dare put those negative things away? Hoping and praying you'll be "stricken" with enough purpose to motivate you to do what's necessary to achieve a healthier and more meaningful life?

If so, I've got news for you...

Your addictions are fooling you into doing this thing backwards.

See, you should NOT wait to find your sense of purpose and motivation before you put down the things which are sapping your spirit and slowly killing your body.

INSTEAD - WALK AWAY FROM THE NEGATIVE BEHAVIORS AND LET YOUR PURPOSE FIND YOU!!

I promise, you DO have a beautiful purpose on this planet.

A purpose which will reassure you that you are meaningful and powerful beyond measure!

And provide more than sufficient motivation to make all those short-term indulgences seem pathetic and uninteresting in comparison.

But finding it is NOT a matter of hoping, praying, or patiently waiting while you meditate by the river.

In fact, your purpose is not something you must actively seek AT ALL.

Your purpose is something you DETECT when you are 100% present for life in a loving and consistent way (Stephen Covey taught me that).

You've got to clear away the muck so you can BE PRESENT FOR YOUR PURPOSE WHEN IT ARRIVES.

Just put down your addiction, look around and see what happens.

Eventually - much sooner than you think -- your purpose will find you.

PURPOSE REQUIRES PRESENCE.

AND ADDICTIONS ARE ITS ENEMY.

DON'T WAIT FOR A PURPOSE TO PUT DOWN YOUR ADDICTION.

PUT DOWN YOUR ADDICTION AND LET YOUR PURPOSE INVADE YOU FROM EVERY ANGLE.

It's there, I promise. You just have to be there long enough to embrace it.

From the Bottom of My Heart to the Bottom of Yours

If you still struggle with food there's something, I want you to know from the bottom of my heart to the bottom of yours. I KNOW YOU CAN FIX THIS.

See, I haven't met anyone who was more in the grips of overeating than myself.

Who spent his days thinking about food.

And his nights buried under a truckload of it.

Who sat by the refrigerator with a chair wondering what was wrong with him.

Who could dislodge his jaw and empty the contents of the delicatessen into it.

I know how bad it can be!

And I also know how simplistic my solution seems on its surface.

But the question I want you all to pose to yourself if you're feeling powerless over food is - could the 2,000+ reviews on Amazon all be lying? If there are 2,000+ people who thought enough to go back to Amazon and leave a review.

Then there must be something to this - it's NOT just me.

Now of course your Pig says "It works for them, but it could never work for us because we are DIFFERENT! Our genetics won't permit it. Glenn doesn't understand your stressful lifestyle. Glenn doesn't have to live with an antagonistic spouse who's constantly eating Pig Slop. Glenn is a 6'4", muscular, active man who can burn a lot of calories and get away with eating a lot of food. Glenn never gains weight in his ass like we do. Glenn lives in a big city with lots of food resources. Glenn is a psychologist. Glenn is really smart. Blah blah blah blah blah"

Listen, I've got 600,000 readers and I've seen hundreds of clients. I've heard it ALL.

Repeat after me: "YOU ARE NOT DIFFERENT."

Everyone's Pig is more or less the same.

You know, when I first started coaching clients on Never Binge Again, I was pretty sure I was going to be overwhelmed with literally thousands of creative Pig Squeals. I thought I'd be inundated and exhausted from trying to figure them all out. But you know what? After several years now, I've yet to identify more than fifty. And I've got answers for them all. I can see the half-truths AND the lies in every single one of them.

YOU ARE NOT DIFFERENT. If you'd like to see me climb up on top of a clock tower and start screaming with aluminum foil on my head, then go ahead and be the nine millionth person who tries to convince me that you are!

Your Pig is more or less the same as everyone else's.

And unless you've had a brain operation to remove your ability to voluntarily control your hands, arms, legs, mouth and tongue, your neurology is more or less the same as everyone else's too.

YOU HAVE THE ABILITY TO CONTROL WHAT GOES IN YOUR MOUTH – JUST LIKE EVERYONE ELSE. No matter what you've heard from the so-called experts in our society. Or especially the 12 step syndicates.

From the bottom of my heart to the bottom of yours I KNOW you can do this!

Hey, here's a thought...

What if I'm right?

A Few Mantras You Can Use When You're Tempted to Overeat

One of the most frequent questions I get from clients is "What can I say to myself in the moment I'm tempted to throw out all my best thinking and overeat and/or binge?" Here are several phrases tested and proven in the trenches hundreds of times with my clients and my readers:

- **"Not One Bite!"**: Reminding yourself never to take even one bite off of your carefully constructed Food Plan helps counter a variety of Pig Squeals like "One bite can't hurt" or "it's only a little bit" or even "we can just start again tomorrow." One bite DOES hurt. It will reinforce the pattern and make it HARDER to eat well tomorrow. One bite can be a tragedy. Not one bite!

- **"I Always Use the Present Moment to Be Healthy"**: Your Inner Pig will try to convince you the present moment doesn't count. Or that no matter what you do in the present it will get you to overeat in the future for one reason or another, so you shouldn't even bother trying to eat well. This mantra takes you right back to NOW, which is the ONLY time you can eat. Always use the present moment to be healthy and you'll always be alright :-)

- **"Every Craving is an Opportunity"**: Every craving IS an opportunity to further extinguish your cravings! See, when you crave something bad but redirect your food intake to something healthy instead, you're setting up a new neurological pathway and making the old one weaker. For example, if I crave pasta but eat a bunch of whole fruit instead, I've begun teaching my survival drive it's supposed to direct its energy towards fruit AND begun detaching its energy from pasta. I couldn't do that without experiencing the pasta craving first! So every craving IS an opportunity -

and when you welcome them, you'll more easily remember how to reprogram yourself to be healthier!

➢ **"If You Have Six Problems and Then You Overeat, Then You'll Have Seven Problems!"** The Pig wants you to believe Pig Slop is the solution to all your problems, but the truth is that overeating only adds more stress to your life. You'll have to digestively recover from it. It can take a week or more to authentically lose the weight it puts on your thighs, hips, belly, and face. Your blood sugar will destabilize, and you'll probably crash and have to spend several low-energy, low-productivity hours, sapping your ability to deal with the original problems. If you have six problems and then you overeat, you'll have seven problems!

➢ **"Feelings Aren't Facts!"** Just because every bone in your body says you need the Pig Slop to survive *(and screams for it at the top of its lungs)* doesn't mean you actually do. The whole purpose of all this industrially engineered food is to bypass your best judgment and make you feel like you "need" it. But you don't! Just because your Mom, Dad, Sister, Best Friend, or Your Dog FEELS you are a weirdo for trying to eat healthy does NOT mean you are. And just because it FEELS like you'll never stop binging and reach your ideal weight does NOT mean that you won't. Feelings aren't facts, facts are facts. And here's one for you: If even one person can binge "uncontrollably" for decades and then stop, then so can you. You are not different. You are NOT! If one person can do it so can another.

➢ **"If You're Going Through Hell – Keep Going!"**: Your Pig will try to say that your troubles will last forever, and the only way out is to sit down and eat some Slop. But the truth is, you CAN walk through them if you just keep walking. So walk away!

➢ **"I Can Eat Anything I Want To TOMORROW":** This

one's a little tricky but very powerful once you understand it. See, the goal of Never Binge Again is to put all your critical eating decisions under the control of your intellect vs. your emotions and your body *(where they've been making trouble to this point!)* We do that vis a vis following a written Food Plan *(a set of Food Rules)* to the letter. But we can CHANGE this plan if we really want to, as long as (a) we write down exactly what the change is and what the new limits are; (b) exactly WHY we're making the change and; (c) provided we wait 24 to 48 hours before allowing the change to take effect.

All three elements of this change strategy are critical. (a) You must know exactly where your bulls-eye begins and ends at all times or else you're playing blind archery. And if you shoot arrows at a not-so-well defined target someone's probably going to get hurt! (b) You must be able to articulate exactly why, in very logical terms, you want to make the change you're about to make. Otherwise your Pig has the opportunity to simply make the change for emotional or *erroneous* physiological reasons. And (c) you must wait at least 24 hours otherwise the Pig can simply make changes willy-nilly for its own pleasure. It also ensures you've got time to seriously consider whether your reasoning in (a) and (b) was correct. *(In every legal system there's usually a period of debate and delay before a new law takes effect – there's a good reason for this!)* One alternative form of this mantra which some people find useful is "It's not that I can't have that, I'm choosing not to!"

➢ **"That's Not Where My Freedom Is!"** Freedom sits on top of discipline, not opposed to it. A jazz pianist can only express their soul in improvisation because they've spent years practicing scales. They can improvise away from the music's structure only because they know where it is and can get back to it at a moment's notice. Your car only extends your freedom and allows you much greater radius of locomotion because of the discipline of the engineers that constructed it such that the wheels would turn exactly 30 degrees when you turn the steering wheel correspondingly. You can drive where you like because of the populace's agreement to stop at red lights and stop signs. Your ability to enjoy food freely and with great satisfaction exists only because you know exactly what to put vs. not to put in your mouth. Your freedom is NOT in Pig Slop, your slavery is! Don't be a slave to your impulses. Stand up and claim your freedom! An alternative to this one is "Every time I say no to Pig Slop I say yes to Freedom!"

➢ **"Hunger Means the Fat is Melting!"** Obviously this one needs to be used within reason, and only when you're intellectually sure your body is well nourished and calorically supplied to no more than a small deficit (losing just one to two pounds per week). And this is something people should use only when they authentically DO need to lose weight! But when this is all the case you can consider feeling proud of your hunger and learning to enjoy it, because you'll need to experience at least a little of it in order to accomplish your physical goals. Something else people do in this situation is grab their fat stores and shout "Let It Burn Baby, Let It Burn!"

➢ **"My Future Self Will Appreciate Me."** Your Pig may be miserable that you're choosing not to eat Slop at the moment, but YOU will be happy you didn't in the future. My Pig has been upset about all sorts of things I didn't eat, but I've never regretted NOT feeding it Slop!

➢ **"That is Not My Food" and/or "That is Not Who I Am Anymore":** I once knew a woman who owned a bakery when she discovered she had to completely avoid feeding her Pig sugar and flour. You might think this was quite a quandary for her since she not only had to be around Slop all day long but had to make it seem sexy to her bakery customers so she could sell it. But she was very successful, so I asked her how she did it. "Simple," she said "I just say 'That is not my food' whenever I feel tempted."

➢ **"Right Now I Choose the Better Way**" And since the future is an infinite string of nows, you will always choose the better way if you adopt this mantra!

➢ **"You Are Trying to Kill Me Pig and I'm On to You!**" Our society seems to have a tacit agreement to slowly kill ourselves with food. We all sit around in restaurants and fast food joints shoveling unnatural concentrations of fat, sugar, salt, starch, and excitotoxins into our face-holes. We make jokes about it. We laugh and support each other to enjoy the experience. But the statistics don't lie – we are indeed killing ourselves with Slop. Don't let your Pig fool you. You're onto that sucker!

➢ **"Every Bite is an Opportunity to Practice Self-Care vs. Self-Harm with Food!"** According to the principles of neuroplasticity we are always either reinforcing or extinguishing our addictions. There is no "treading water" or "standing still." So "start again" tomorrow is bogus – if you dig the groove deeper today you'll have a harder time getting the train moving in the right direction tomorrow. But if you start NOW tomorrow will be easier. Every moment is an opportunity for self-care vs. self-harm with food. Which will you choose?

➢ **"Damn the Man!"** When craving some kind of manufactured junk say 'Damn The Man', as in damn the big corporations with their targeted, over-engineered food. Refuse to give them your money or the satisfaction that they have you addicted to their bags, boxes, and containers. Use the rebel inside you—*the same one that use to try to get you to* *break your food plan—to* help you stick to it. “Damn the Man!”

➢ **“I Don’t Eat See Food!”:** Just plan out your meals beforehand for a day and stick to the plan. Whenever your Pig throws a craving at you for something off-plan which shows up in your visual field say "I never eat see food" and go on with your planned meal. Don’t eat see food!!!

➢ **“There’s NO Doctor Out There Diagnosing a Sugar and/or Flour Deficiency!”** Need I say more?

Finally, the last two mantras below are intended specifically for when you’re tempted by what your spouse, partner, children, and/or significant other is eating, doing, or saying:

➢ **“Run Your Own Race”:** Remember, everyone’s diet/food-plan is entirely up to them. One person’s Pig Slop is another person’s healthy treat, regardless of whether they’ve read Never Binge Again. Your Pig would have you get VERY involved in what the other person is eating. It wants you to feel deprived, rather than focus on what eating Pig Slop deprives you of *(energy, healthy, productivity, presence of mind, life!).* It wants you to feel things are incredibly unfair. That you SHOULD be able to eat anything in moderation, especially what other people are eating. It would have you rip every last bite of your significant other’s Slop out of their hands (and whatever remained in their mouth) to gulp it down yourself. Screw that Squeal! Live your own life. Run your own race. Just get on with it!

➢ **“This Train is Leaving the Station”** Stop waiting for your significant other to eat healthy and/or exercise before you do. I know it would be easier if they would, but you don’t need them to do it. Be a leader. Get on the train and let it leave the station. They can come if they want to or stay home and eat Slop. The odds are they’ll be more influenced by your results over the course of six months to a year vs. any words you may use to try and convince them. Go get those results. Let the train leave the station!

Finally, if you're tired of breaking your best laid food plans time and again, sick of the bloating, painful digestion, excess weight, and demoralization associated with binge eating and/or overeating, and you'd like to have more mantras and more personal help to overcome your cravings, please visit...

www.NeverBingeAgainCoaching.com

The Consciously and Purposefully Clause for Your Food Plan

Here's something I should've put in the original book but didn't...

I consider every rule in my Food Plan to be preceded by the words "Consciously and Purposefully".

For example, when I say "I Will Never Eat Chocolate Again!" what I really mean is "I Will Never Consciously and Purposefully Eat Chocolate Again!"

This prevents the Pig from taking advantage of genuine accidents.

For example, I was once in a Mexican restaurant and noticed I was feeling just a little too happy after eating my dish. The feeling was a little too familiar – something like I'd felt during my chocolate binges but of much lower intensity.

So, I asked the waiter what was in the dish.

And lo and behind there WAS chocolate as an ingredient. He said "Not much but a little."

Did I panic? Did I break my Food Plan?

Well even if I HAD that wouldn't be a reason to panic because what you're supposed to do the minute you realize you've broken your plan is get right back on it. None of this "free until the end of the day" prairie pooh, right!?

But the truth is, I did NOT break my Food Plan, because I didn't consciously and purposefully eat chocolate. If I'd decided to order seconds or take another bite of whatever was left on my plate then I WOULD have broken it, but I didn't.

This turns out to be a very helpful rule for many people in situations where they genuinely did accidentally ingest something off their plan.

Why Lying To Yourself About Food Can Be a Good Thing!

TRUE OR FALSE? Lying to yourself about your diet is always a bad thing. False! There's one specific instance where keeping secrets from yourself can be an incredibly powerful way to stick to it. Indulge me for a few minutes and you might just find you've got more control than you've previously thought.

Let's start out with something I said to my precious niece Sarah when she was only two years old. "Sarah", I said, "You can never ever EVER cross the street without holding my hand, OK? Never, do you understand?" (She did.) But here's the thing - I lied to her. I knew full well when she was older she'd be taught how to carefully look both ways, but I consciously and purposefully lied to her anyway.

Was I an evil uncle? No! I did it to protect her! A two-year-old is nowhere near mature enough to even entertain the thought of darting into a busy street by herself. I didn't want that image in her head. I didn't want her distracted by any stretch of the imagination. I wanted her to concentrate 100% of her energies on crossing the street successfully with her hand firmly gripping mine. That was the task at hand, and the mindset required for a two-year-old to accomplish it was the total and complete purging of any thoughts to the contrary. So, I kept my future plans for her a secret. I said "Never" as if it were set in stone. I did not say "Sarah, when you're a few years older I'll teach you to look both ways and cross by yourself." I lied and if the situation were presented to me again, I'd do it again in a heartbeat!

Your Dieting Mind Acts Like a Two Year Old

The problem with sticking to a diet is, in essence, our reptilian brain, the seat of primitive survival reactions. Fight or flight. Feast or famine. This is where the feeling of "Who cares about my diet, I simply must eat this now!" comes from. That's why there are jokes like "hand over the chocolate and nobody gets hurt". We all intuitively understand those moments where it seems like none of our previous commitments matter. We let our biology take over and say "screw it." Our reptilian brain is like a two-year-old when it comes to sticking to a diet. And the big food and advertising industries are all too happy to provide hyper-palatable concentrations of starch, sugar, fat, oil, sodium, and excitotoxins to coax your reptilian brain out into the street by itself!

To fix this, you've got to take control of your reptilian brain and force it to hold your hand when you eat and/or are faced with temptation - which is everywhere in our modern food environment. You don't want it even thinking about breaking the rules. That way you can purge all the doubt and uncertainty from your mind and concentrate all your energy on achieving your weight loss, health, and fitness goals.

To Finally Lose Weight You Might Have to Keep Secrets From Yourself

What's the dietary equivalent of presenting a "you may never ever cross the street without holding my hand" rule to a two year old? It's actually pretty simple. Make a food rule, any food rule, and pretend like it's set in stone. Tell your reptilian brain, for example "I will never eat pizza except for Saturdays again!"

You know you can change this rule at any time. It would be silly, for example, to stick to it if a whole slew of scientifically valid, sound, and replicated studies came out documenting incontrovertible health benefits of eating pizza every day. That's probably not going to happen, but the point is you're always learning and maturing. What you think of as a healthy diet necessarily needs to be able to evolve as you accumulate more wisdom, knowledge, and experience.

But your reptilian brain doesn't need to know that! You can keep a secret from yourself about it so the reptilian brain isn't constantly tempted, and so you don't have to make decisions in the moment. *(Decisions wear down your willpower).* You can "act as if" your "I will only ever eat pizza on Saturdays again" is a rule you've set in stone until at least one second after the end of the universe arrives.

It's a great way to kill that annoying chatter in your head: "Maybe I could have some today, even though it's a Wednesday, because I worked out so hard at the gym", "I could make up for it by juice fasting tomorrow", "a few bites won't hurt", "I'll start my diet again tomorrow", etc.

You know you could change your rule to allow pizza on Wednesdays, but you're not going to do it impulsively. You'll give yourself 48 hours after writing down exactly why and how you want to change that rule. This way you're protected from the reptilian brain's impulses, and you've moved your decision making about your diet from your emotions to your intellect without restricting yourself from having anything you really want in the future. You can change your food plan anytime you want to - you just won't allow your reptilian brain to do it for you in the moment!

Go ahead, try it. Keep just one secret from yourself for just one week. I know it's weird, but what if I'm right? *(Read Never Binge Again for free to really understand how to do this!)*

Don't Eat Bugs (How to Stop Lying to Yourself About Food!)

One day about thirty years ago, my ex-wife and I were staying at my parents' house in Cold Spring Harbor, NY. Sharon had woken up earlier than I did so she went downstairs to join my Dad for breakfast alone, and she found him there eating a great big bowl of oatmeal.

WITH ABOUT A HUNDRED ANTS CRAWLING IN IT!

"Marty!" she screamed.

"Put on your glasses! There are ANTS crawling in your oatmeal!" she gasped.

"Those aren't ants, those are RAISINS!" my Dad said with confidence, as he continued gulping down spoonful after spoonful.

"No Marty! They are f-----------g ANTS!!!" she said again.

But dad kept right on eating, so she quietly walked away feeling a bit nauseous, and left him to feast on his buggy oatmeal by himself. She later told me "If he doesn't want to know then he doesn't want to know!"

Now here's the thing.

YOU should want to know.

I'm sure you're not eating bugs. Well, at least I'm PRETTY sure.

But if your Pig is anything like mine, I'll bet you've eaten a lot of other stuff you'd IMMEDIATELY recognize didn't belong in your body if you took a closer look. Here's how mine used to lie to me:

- Glenn, you know all the salt in those beans at that fast food restaurant doesn't matter so much because at least the beans are low glycemic. *(Ignoring the fact that excess sodium risks a hemorrhagic stroke even if I didn't have high blood pressure and that there's an exceedingly high risk of this in my cardiovascular genetics)*

- *"Hey Bubba (my Pig calls me Bubba, I'm not really sure why)* That dark chocolate bar has fabulous antioxidants in it!" *(Ignoring the fact it's also got a ridiculous amount of sugar and stimulants in it which have historically caused me to eat 3,000+ more calories than I need on any given day).*

- You need the protein in that big mound of peanut-butter *(ignoring the fact that overdoing fat in my diet has historically raised my triglycerides and predisposed me to diabetes!)*

- *Etc.*

You get the idea!

It's a big problem to focus on the good part of a "food" while completely ignoring the harmful ingredients and/or effects.

DON'T IGNORE THE ANTS!

Behind Every Fear is a Wish

Shssssssssssssshhhhhhhh...I've got a secret for over-eaters which can REALLY help. But don't let your Pig know OK? My great big secret is:

"Behind Every Fear is a Wish"

Within this simple secret lies THE lever you can pull to stop the binge eating train in its tracks. But you have to have an open mind. You have to at least be willing to CONSIDER it, because after all, I just might be right.

OK, now here's the thing, When you are AFRAID ON ANY LEVEL that you might break your Food Plan and Binge, What's really going on is you're experiencing your Pig's WISH to Binge. It's NOT really a fear, it's a wish! See, binge anxiety is the first sign that the Pig is trying to fool you into thinking its thoughts are your own, but if you remember "behind every fear is a wish" and "I'm NOT afraid I might binge, the Pig just really, really WANTS to binge," you'll be more thoroughly committed to the separation of your constructive vs. destructive thoughts with food, and you'll be giving yourself those crucial extra microseconds at the moment of impulse which allow you to wake up and remember who you are so you can make the right decision.

Changing your language to switch out fears for wishes restores your sense of agency and power. It reminds you that the CHOICE is yours, as it always has been.

You're NOT afraid You might Binge, your Inner Pig just really really WANTS to Binge.

Don't believe me? Try it anyway and see what happens.

Getting Comfortable Sticking to Your Food Plan

The two most popularly highlighted paragraphs in my #1 bestselling book "Never Binge Again" *(available FREE at www.NeverBingeAgain.com)* may seem contradictory. The first one says:

> "When you care enough, tolerating any level of discomfort

FOREVER is suddenly within your power. No matter how strong a craving your Inner Pig(tm) might throw at you"

This comes right after a thought experiment in the book which suggested that if the life of the person you cherished most in the world were suddenly dependent upon you not eating this or that, you certainly could avoid eating this or that as long as it took. Because suddenly the IMPORTANCE of staying on your Food Plan was jacked WAY UP!

The conclusion of this section suggested we must all, at some point, inform our Pig we are willing to tolerate ANY level of discomfort, whether emotional or physical, to stay on our plan! *(Something I emphatically believe.)*

But the OTHER most popularly highlighted paragraph focuses on the exact opposite - staying comfortable!:

"Humans are wired to seek sustenance as a major priority in three situations: (1) when nutrients are depleted; (2) when we get too cold and; (3) when our blood sugar drops too low. Sometimes, we also confuse dehydration with hunger. Therefore: You can keep the discomfort associated with cravings to a minimum by staying relatively warm and hydrated, and consuming regular, consistent, healthy meals. Most people can almost totally eliminate the physiological experience of cravings when they attend to these elements of self-care."

Is there a contradiction?

NO!

See, I am NOT promoting a masochistic approach to life. I WANT you to be comfortable.

I want you to do what's necessary to take excellent care of your body. I do NOT want you to overly restrict your food, calories, or nutrition.

But sometimes life throws us a curve ball. You've got to take a meeting instead of eating your planned lunch. Your kid gets hurt and you've got to run to school to pick them up. Your elderly parent has a problem and the two hours you THOUGHT you had free to prepare a healthy dinner just vanishes.

Stuff happens!

Sh___t gets in the way.

And sometimes you have to tolerate a little (or a lot) of physical and/or emotional discomfort without indulging in unhealthy eating behaviors.

Your Pig needs to know you're willing to do that, no matter what!

At the same time you can and should do everything you can to take good care of yourself. Feed your body right. Avoid UNNECESSARY discomfort.

Because there's NO point in giving the Pig ANY extra ammunition or credence when it says "Oh c'mon already, we're going to STARVE if we don't eat that Pig Slop!" The net-net is, people who struggle with binge eating and overeating need to take exceptionally good care of their physical needs. Stay hydrated, warm, and be sure you get more than adequate nutrition throughout the day. But simultaneously warn your Pig that in the event something interferes with this, you're willing to tolerate ANY level of discomfort without straying from your carefully constructed Food Plan!

I hope that makes sense!

Accelerating Your Metabolism to Lose Weight

I had an interesting conversation with a client about special "miracle" pills from India that apparently accelerate your metabolism. His personal trainer told him they do wonders. So, we hopped on the internet and checked them out. And after a few minutes we discovered that only miracle these pills create is acute diarrhea, which means they'll dehydrate you and prevent you from digesting food so you'd be practically starving yourself!

Yes, you'll lose weight, but you'll damage your health in the process.

I'm sorry to be the one to tell you this but...

THERE IS NO FREE LUNCH!

No weight loss teas, pills, detox-shakes or voodoo masters can shortcut your way to losing weight without causing damage. The only thing that works to lose the weight and achieve your health and fitness goals, as well as to dramatically build up your self-esteem and confidence is changing your eating habits for good.

If and when I find another way, if I discover a truly magical pill, or a diet that lets you have your cake and eat it too, just leave me your contact info and I PROMISE I'll get in touch with you immediately. Even if I'm smack in the middle of eating a raw food salad with Rosie O'Donnell while teaching her how to yodel!

What To Do When Every Cell In Your Body Says "Binge, Binge, Binge!"

It's my firm belief most people who struggle with overeating have accidentally triggered an evolutionary mechanism in their brain by putting themselves through periods of dieting and/or restrictive eating in the past. There seems to be something hard-wired into our neurology which says "look, we obviously live in an environment where calories and nutrients can be scarce for long periods of time we therefore must hoard them whenever they ARE available!"

Of course, Big Food is all too happy to throw their billions into researching the best ways to cram as much fat, sugar, salt, calories, and stimulants into the smallest space possible, then billions more to package it up it so it LOOKS healthy. While the addiction treatment industry screams "you're powerless to resist!" and the advertising industry beams 7,000+ messages about food at us each year with almost NONE of them being about fruit and vegetables!

With all this pressure on our survival drive is it any wonder we ALL feel, at times, as if a binge is inevitable? No, we all face moments where every cell in our body seems to be screaming for a binge. What can we do? How can we fight evolution AND the three industries with enormous profit incentives to push our evolutionary buttons?

It's actually NOT as difficult as it seems:

- ➢ **First, make sure your Food Plan is sufficient in both calories and nutrition**. Do NOT try to lose weight too quickly - in my experience this ALWAYS backfires. *(Similarly, make up for a binge with a week of regular, normal, healthy eating. Not several days where you hardly eat at all. Eat a healthy breakfast the morning after a binge even if you don't feel like it. Teach your body that normal, healthy food is always available, so there's really no need to hoard.)*

- ➢ **Thoroughly assess your trigger foods and eating behaviors.** There aren't as many as your Inner Pig(tm) would have you believe. Then focus on the one or two which are REALLY giving you a run for the money, and make a crystal clear rule which defines how you will behave around those foods and/or situations.

➢ REMEMBER: **Willpower is a muscle proven to fatigue as the day wears on. There are only so many good DECISIONS you can make in a day.** But CHARACTER commitments require no energy or willpower at all. Character commitments allow you to make your important food decisions beforehand, so they don't wear down your willpower muscle as the day progresses. It takes NOT willpower to leave the waitress's tip sitting on the table when you walk into the diner even when nobody's there to see because you've already committed to being a law-abiding member of society.

As a matter of character, you are NOT a thief. Similarly, you can commit to becoming the kind of person who only eats chocolate on weekends, never eats in front of the TV, always eats six servings of fruit and vegetables every day, etc. Character trumps impulse and it CAN beat the immense power of Big Food, Big Advertising, and Big Addiction Treatment combined.

➢ **If the urge to binge is too strong, eat some more HEALTHY calories and nutrients right away.** You might not lose weight that day *(or you may even be up a little the next)* but you won't have to recover from the Binge, and you'll be training your body that it's not necessary to worry about starvation, therefore it can begin to let go of those nasty biological urges to binge. So, fill up on a food from the UNLIMITED category of your Food Plan. One of my friends and a very smart practitioner of the NBA system eats 3-4 cucumbers and a bit of low-fat yogurt when he's really hungry. He finds this particular combination tasty and extremely effective in quieting his cravings. Now, putting low fat yogurt in the unlimited category may not work for everyone, but you get the point. Find your own UNLIMITED "go to" food and add a reminder something to effect of: 'I may eat 4 cucumbers and 4 ounces of low-fat yogurt at any time.'

➢ **Remember the principle of neuroplasticity which states: "That which fires together wires together!"** This means the way you treat every single urge to binge will either reinforce your addiction...or extinguish it. The urge will either stronger or weaker next time depending upon your choice. Every bite you put in your mouth is an opportunity for self-love vs. self-harm. Choose self-love... because ultimately, you've only got one self!

➢ **If you STILL think you really have to binge right now, remind yourself it's NOT you, it's your Pig!** YOU want to be healthy, thin and energetic but the Pig doesn't care about any of that. It only cares for its Slop and it will sacrifice ALL your hopes, dreams, relationships, and EVERYTHING you care about to get it. So get REALLY mad at the Pig's attack. Instead of surrendering, attack back, telling it, essentially, to go screw! "The heck with you Pig! You want me to destroy my health, my body and my life just so you can get a bit of your freaking Slop! I've just showed you who's boss. I'm not hungry. You failed! Go back to your damn cage right now and shut up. GO NOW!" *(It sounds crazy, but you can think of this as your opportunity to get back at the Pig for all the years it made you suffer. And because it can be difficult to access your rational brain when the fight-or-flight response kicks in during binge-mode, using this kind of a visceral response can be a lot more practical. Think of yourself as an alpha wolf being challenged for leadership by another member of the pack. When this happens, the Alpha does NOT say "Awwwwwe, does somebody need a hug!?" Essentially what it does is snarl and growl and bear its teeth as if to say "Get back in line or I'll kill you!" That's the attitude you want to have to get the Pig back in its Cage. You can't actually kill it, but you can scare the hell out of it. And because it's neurologically the inferior animal, it WILL be frightened of you and submit if you want it to and you show it you mean business!)*

The Leafy Greens Trick for Binge Recovery

Hey! I'd much prefer you used the Never Binge Again method to, well, Never Binge Again! That said, people DO make mistakes. So, I wanted to share a quick little tip to help you get back on track after a binge, or even just a little overeating mistake. See, most people don't binge on broccoli, they binge on industrially engineered foods: Bags, containers, and boxes of things which did NOT exist on the Savannah or in the tropics millions of years ago when humans first appeared.

The problem is, these bags, boxes, and containers produce an artificial pleasure we are NOT evolutionarily prepared to handle. They kind of short-circuit our neurological pleasure systems and HIJACK our survival drive, so that instead of craving whole, fresh, natural foods, we come to THINK we literally can't survive without Big Food's over-engineered food-like-substances. And of course, this is just how they like it. Your Pig is their best customer!

Unfortunately, what happens right after a Binge is that your brain gets busy rewiring itself to profit those fat cat executives by craving those bags, boxes, and containers even more strongly than it did beforehand.

But you do NOT have to let this happen! What you CAN do immediately after a binge is feed your body something healthy. Something it genuinely DOES need to survive.

The one thing I've found which most diets CAN agree on as healthy is LEAFY GREEN VEGETABLES. So, unless you have a medical condition which prevents you from doing so *(check with your doctor first)*, consider stuffing a half pound of leafy green vegetables in a blender with some water after a binge.

Resist the urge to put in any powders, potions, or supplements. Just blend up the darn thing and drink it down like medicine.

You'll likely find yourself immediately more confident in your ability to get back on track!

Why? It feels magical but it's not that mysterious. Our bodies evolved eating leafy greens, so by introducing them in the middle of the toxic-rewiring of your post-binge brain you are PHYSIOLOGICALLY INTERRUPTING the addictive process and reminding your brain what it SHOULD crave instead.

It's really that simple.

Don't believe me? You don't have to. Just try it!

Oh - and you don't have to wait until you have a Binge either.

If you want to recover from your cravings faster you can do this BEFORE a binge too.

As a matter of fact, with the exception of some very rare medical conditions I'm not sure if there's ANY doctor out there who'd object to people adding a half pound of leafy greens to their diet each day. *(Which reminds me - I've never heard of any doctor telling their patients to eat MORE flour and sugar. "The reason you're sick Ms. Jones is because you don't have enough refined flour and sugar in your diet. Go visit the donut shop immediately" - yeah, that's not something you hear in the waiting room).*

Anyway, that's the leafy greens trick for binge recovery, for what it's worth. And it's worth a LOT!

The Food Craving Journal

Here's a really cool, VERY practical technique to kill stubborn cravings: Just write them down! Keep a pen and paper handy at all times *(or use the Notes app on your smart phone)* and then, when the craving hits, put it in black and white and tell yourself you'll figure out what to do about it later.

This does two things:

- **First, it takes you out of "fight or flight" mode and stops you from acting NOW.** And since now is the only time you can ever binge, and the future is an infinite string of "Nows", if you don't binge NOW, you'll Never Binge Again!
- **Secondly, you'll start to see a pattern, which makes it easier to figure out how to substitute for the craving.** For example, I remember craving three things over and over again (1) pasta with tomato sauce and cheese and; (2) pizza; (3) grilled cheese sandwiches. See the pattern? Starchy + salty + cheesy. I eventually figured out I could have brown rice, tomato sauce, and nutritional yeast to kill that craving. That was SO much healthier than what I'd been doing! Then (a few years later) I substituted zuchinni and/or cucumber noodles for the brown rice. Then homemade, sodium free tomato sauce, etc. Granted, these substitutions never "got me high" with food the same way the pizza and pasta and bagels did, but I got much healthier and it became EASY to deal with the cravings!

It's so simple, most people overlook it. Don't!

Sugar, Flour, and Alcohol

If you've tried "everything" to stop overeating and it's just "not working" *(your Pig's language, not mine), try this:* Switch to a Food Plan with ZERO sugar, flour, or alcohol for thirty days. You can decide if you want to reintegrate these substances with very specific boundaries after that point *(with careful consideration and evaluation of your results).*

But zeroing out sugar, flour, and alcohol has worked virtual miracles for SO many clients I can't help but mention it. These substances create cravings for themselves and interfere not only with your blood chemistry, but your judgment and impulse control across many areas of life.

Try ZERO sugar, flour, and alcohol for thirty days. You might be surprised how well it works for you!

Salty, Crunchy Snacks

I was curious to know which foods people struggled with the most these days, so I commissioned a 2800+ person study with a representative sample of the united states population, and I discovered something which really surprised me! When I asked what food categories most felt they couldn't stop eating when they started, the #1 answer by far was "salty crunchy snacks".

In fact 3x as many people struggle with chips, pretzels, and other crunchy salty things as compared to chocolate! A previous study I did suggested that the people who are prone to binging on chips, pretzels, and other salty crunchy snacks tend to be those who were more stressed at work.

Makes you think twice about eating that first chip doesn't it? Especially if your job is stressing you out or your boss is an idiot! None of this means you're powerless to stop however, I promise. Just some sobering stats to make you think twice.

You Probably Don't Need Any New Information to Lose Weight

YOU DON'T ALWAYS NEED NEW INFORMATION TO CHANGE: Sometimes I catch myself waiting to learn something NEW and/or figure out something NEW to do when what I really need to do is just the obvious. For example, over the winter I was eating too many dates and my weight crept up a few pounds. But, because I didn't want to accept this fact - (because I f****g love dates!) - the little voice inside me that compelled me to find some NEW nutritional information to lose weight was very alluring.

I bought some books.

Started reading.

But all I really needed to do was just let go of the damn dates for a while and poof, the weight started dropping again.

So now I ask myself before I start info-seeking "What do I ALREADY KNOW that I'm not doing?"

The answer is usually right under our nose.

A Simple Technique to Shut Down Binge Thinking Before It Starts

What if you could PREVENT binge eating thoughts before they happened?

In the classic rapper movie "8-Mile", Eminem won his rap battle using a very weird technique, one YOU can use to shut your Pig up before it says one word! Here's what Eminem said in his Rap:

> "I know everything he's got to say against me...
> I AM white...
> I AM a freaking Bum...
> I DO live in a trailer with my Mum...
> My boy Future IS an Uncle Tom...
> I DO have a dumb friend named Cheddar Bob...
> Who shoots himself in his leg with his own gun"

And by the time Eminem is finished listing his OWN faults, the battle is won because he's exposed everything bad about himself first, leaving his poor opponent with NO ammunition.

One of my clients used a very similar technique to silence her own Pig before it had a chance to get the better of her:

> "I've been journaling every day to get any Pig Squeals out of the way first thing in the morning. This was working pretty well. Except now the Pig doesn't have much to say. I think it is waiting to catch me in a moment of weakness (I realize that this very thought is Pig Squeal, lol).
>
> Anyway, even though my Pig is quiet. That is good. It means my Pig finally shut up and has nothing compelling to say to me. It has been much easier to stick to my plan."

Like our students, you too can release yourself from the clutches of binge eating and overeating thoughts by challenging your Pig each and every morning to give you its best reason for you to overeat/binge. This completely removes the element of surprise and gives you a chance to consider what's illogical in the Pig's reasoning. *(The Pig always relies on half-truths combined with a logical fallacy).*

It's very empowering – and you don't have to take my word for it, just try!

Stopping Stealthy Binges That Creep Up On You

A thought like: "Hey, it's midnight, time to eat 6 slices of pizza and that yummy bar of chocolate" is an obviously binge motivated thought, and once you recognize it you can just tell your Pig to shut up and send it right back to its cage. That's not what this is about. The problem for most people is that not every binge thought is as obvious as this one. And so, a lot of people experience binges "creeping up" on them, in fact, that's your Pig's most effective tool.

Maybe it all starts with an itsy-bitsy cookie that's served with your coffee. Then there's an office party, and after all, you can't insult Janet from accounting on her birthday, so you'll need to eat at least a few bites of cake. Then on the way home you stop to do your shopping, but because the sugar-high from the cookie and cake turned into an insulin-crash, you now feel exhausted, so you eat a cupcake (or two) in the car, which makes things feel better for about 18 minutes before it makes them much worse. By the time you get home your Pig is already whispering *"Hey... we blew it today... we weren't even close to eating the way we planned... so screw it... let's have a big hairy binging party and just start again tomorrow!"*

That's how one itsy-bitsy coffee-cookie turns into a raging binge. And this kind of "creeping binge" is a lot more common than you think. See, your Pig LOVES that first little cookie because it knows it'll induce the sugar-high and subsequent insulin-crash that allows it to hijack your judgement.

But there's a very simple way to prevent it. You just have to revamp your rules. Sometimes a non-restrictive conditional will do it. For example, "I will never eat a cookie with my coffee again."

See, Food Rules in the Never Binge Again program serve a VERY important purpose, they make it possible to identify every last binge eating thought BEFORE they can escalate into a binge. Even the teeniest, tiniest binge thought, like having a cookie when you shouldn't, or a few bites of birthday cake to please a friend at the office.

Food Rules are NOT there to deprive you of the foods you like, after all it's YOU who gets to decide upon them. 100%! But if you define your Food Rules well, they can protect you from slipping down that creepy crawly slope into a full-fledged binge EVERY SINGLE TIME. *And it's not always necessary to give up a food completely, often just very specifically defining the boundaries in which you may have it is enough!*

Just Live with the Memories

When I was a boy my mother used to be sure there was a whole box of Chocolate Fudge Pop Tarts waiting in the cupboard for me every morning. And I'd eat the WHOLE box, every single morning. She'd also be sure there was a whole case of Coca Cola in the house on a weekly basis, and a box of Sugar Pops every afternoon when I got home.

The thing is, when I was a boy, I COULD eat these things. Not that they were good for me by any stretch of the imagination *(and, sorry Mom, you know I LOVE you but what in the world were you thinking!?).* Nor would I argue in any way that I was developing healthy eating habits. I don't think I ate a vegetable until I was 22 years old. But my metabolism was high, I was VERY active, and my pancreas hadn't worn down its ability to deal with all that refined sugar yet.

See, when we're young, we CAN put our body to war with food and win. But as we age, we lose more and more of those battles. It takes longer and longer to recover from the Slop, and each battle begins to do more permanent damage, until at some point you've got to say to yourself "Part of aging gracefully is coming to terms with the fact life is NOT one big food party. The price I pay for indulging in Slop is SO much worse than not having it - I THINK I WILL JUST LIVE WITH THE MEMORIES"

It's perfectly OK that I have fond memories of eating Pop Tarts, Sugar Pops, and drinking Coca Cola every day. It's just not OK to re-enact the party. Those things are Slop for me now. The past is the past and I don't want to rush into battle without the appropriate armor. I simply can't put my body at war with them anymore and expect to live a long and healthy life without suffering.

THE MEMORIES OF MY FOOD PARTIES ARE SO MUCH BETTER

THAN REENACTING THEM WILL EVER BE.

I completely accept that now. And there's an immeasurable peace that comes with that which I can just barely describe.

I'm indebted to Douglas Graham, author of The 80-10-10 Diet for teaching me this.

Adversity, Optimism, and Character Building

MUST ADVERSITY KILL YOUR SPIRIT?

In the 3 years prior to writing this book I (a) suddenly had to divorce after a 28 year marriage and close down all my businesses except the one that housed Never Binge Again; (b) lost my dog and best friend for 14 years; (c) lost my Mom to ovarian cancer; (d) moved four times, including twice across the country by myself.

And sometimes I have to admit I walk around feeling sorry for myself given all I've been through. But the day I wrote these words was NOT one of those days!

See, I met a VERY special little girl who left a lasting impression on me. She's not quite a teenager, yet she's been through more drama and trauma than most middle aged adults like me and come through the other side with an astounding perspective, and a smile as big as her heart: "I'm glad I went through it all" she said, "because now all the little problems I'll face in life won't seem like anywhere near as big a deal!"

Imagine that - a little girl who not only understand how adversity builds character, but eagerly embraces it with a wide-eyed smile. Some kids you just know are destined to change the world!

Contrast this to your Pig's attitude to adversity which says "Life utterly and completely sucks except for Pig Slop, what more can you expect?"

It's worth remembering this little story when you feel like adversity is killing your spirit. Because it really doesn't have to!

Onwards and Upwards!

Disturbing Things Glenn Does in Restaurants

One day, sometime in 1994 I think, I was having dinner with my Dad in a nice Indian restaurant in the east village of New York City. I distinctly remember the QUIET atmosphere with carpeting on the walls, not too many tables, and lush decorations throughout. I was wearing a cashmere sweater, the bread was on Dad's side of the table, and between he and I was a burning candle.

Now, my Dad is a little deaf so when I asked him to pass the bread, he just kept staring down at his plate and buttering his slice. So, I repeated the request to no avail. After the third try I gave up and reached over the burning candle to get it myself.

AND MY ENTIRE ARM LIT UP IN FLAMES!!

But ONLY for an instant.

During which I yelled at the top of my lungs "F---------K!" while shaking my arm as violently as I could to put out the fire as quickly as it'd started.

Absolutely NOBODY in the entire restaurant saw the flames on the thin filament of my cashmere sweater's right arm. The ONLY thing they saw was a 32 year old man spontaneously yelling "F-------K" for NO apparent reason in a quiet restaurant!

I thought I was going to die, but I just quietly went on with my dinner after explaining what happened to the waiter, who paid extra special attention to my needs the rest of the evening :-)

Why did I tell you this story?

Many of my clients who successfully stop overeating during their normal daily routines get very thrown at restaurants. The trick to overcoming this usually involves making a special request of the waiter, waitress, or chef. I tell my clients to look beyond the specific entrees and dishes offered on the menu, scan the INGREDIENTS within those dishes, and ask for a SPECIAL dish which suits their unique dietary needs. *(For example, if you see a steak house has portobello steak, chicken parmesan, and Caesar salad listed on the menu, that means they have portobello mushrooms, romaine lettuce, and chicken in stock. So, you can ask for big romaine salad dish with mushrooms and grilled chicken. It's not rocket science)*

Most of my clients, however, object to this approach on the grounds they don't want to look like a weirdo. Some even say they "couldn't survive" the experience.

Well, the next time you're worried about that just think of my little restaurant incident. Because if this sophisticated doctor can survive yelling a big giant curse in the middle of a quiet Indian restaurant, you can definitely survive the "weirdness" of a special request. Odds are actually that you'll find the staff in most restaurants VERY interested in helping you because catering to special requests is a GREAT way to create loyal customers!

This little restaurant memory also helps me, by the way, in Holiday Gatherings, with friends, at a business meeting and anywhere else I might be tempted to feel like it'd be too weird to take care of my special food needs.

9 Non-Disgusting Things You Can Eat Instead Of Binging

An important part of the Never Binge Again Food Plan is the UNLIMITED food category. Just knowing that you have, within your reach, a food that you can eat your fill of without breaking your diet, tends to calm people down. And, sometimes, you DO need to actually fill up on something in order to calm down the cravings. But some people find things like Celery or Kale to be absolutely disgusting. Just the thought of eating a cup turns their stomach!

So here are 9 suggestions for things you MAY be able to fill up on *(depending upon your Food Plan)* without ruining your diet. Please remember I'm not a medical doctor and/or licensed dietitian, so this is just a lay person's thoughts on something which may or may not be useful to you:

- ➢ Steamed Broccoli with a tiny bit of sea salt
- ➢ Bell Peppers
- ➢ Cabbage
- ➢ Steamed Cauliflower with a tiny bit of sea salt
- ➢ Tomatoes
- ➢ Cucumbers
- ➢ Leafy greens *(lettuce, spinach, etc)*
- ➢ Water
- ➢ Green tea

Some of these are almost calorie negative *(leafy greens, cabbage, cucumbers, green tea and water)*. Others have a few more calories -- so for some people it may not be smart to drink a tomato juice smoothie every hour or eat three pounds of steamed cauliflower...but a cup full of tomatoes and 3 cucumbers is usually fine (for most people). Now, just decide which of these foods to add to your shopping list and you're done!

The 9 Best Ways to Stop Overeating

You might want to take some notes on this one because you'll find my nine best insights on how to stop overeating below!

1. **Commit with perfection but forgive yourself with dignity.** Winners pursue a goal with an "I will be successful come hell or high water" mentality, NOT a "maybe I will and maybe I won't" attitude. This way they can purge their minds of doubt and insecurity, which would only serve to drain energy from the pursuit of their goal. If they don't make it, however, they analyze what went wrong, make any necessary adjustments in their aim, and then quickly & completely forgive themselves. This way they don't lose any unnecessary energy to self-castigation and negative thinking.

2. **Keep getting up no matter what, no matter what, no matter what!** The name of the game is staying in the game until you win the game. Never ever ever ever ever ever EVER give up! *(Research shows people who get thin and stay thin have many more attempts behind them.)*

3. **Let it burn, baby, let it burn!** We've talked about this earlier in the book but let's include it here for completeness in the 9 ways list: If you're going to lose weight, sometimes you're going to be hungry. Fact of life. As long as you know that (a) you're not getting too thin *(ask your doctor);* (b) you've got sufficient calories and nutrients to sustain you in your daily Food Plan *(if you don't you'll be setting yourself up for a rebound binge);* (c) you aren't anorexic and; (d) you're not losing more than 2 pounds per week... then you want to learn to ENJOY your hunger. Grab your belly, your thighs, or

your butt and say "let it burn, baby!"

4. **Nourish!** For everything you take out of your diet, try to ADD something nourishing. For example, when I quit chocolate I had the intuition I needed kale juice and banana smoothies. Within six weeks I was craving THEM instead of chocolate bars. As crazy as it sounds, behind your craving for salami might be a craving for broccoli and raw almonds. It won't feel like this at first but if you stick with it, you'll thank me. *(I'm not advocating broccoli and almonds per se', just illustrating the principle - you can figure out the healthier substitute for yourself.)*

5. **Tell your Pig it does NOT have a time machine**. We talked about this one before too but it bears repeating here: Just because you always broke your plan in the past doesn't mean you're always going to Pig Out in the future. There IS such a thing as a last time. People grow up and leave all sorts of partying behind them. All you have to do to make that happen is NEVER BINGE NOW because it's always now.

   Even as you read these words and come to the period on this sentence, it is still NOW. When you began reading it, it was now, it's now NOW, and when you're done it will still be NOW. The future is an infinite string of NOWs - therefore, if you NEVER BINGE NOW you will Never Binge Again. Get it?

6. **Commit**. Make clear rules that define what healthy eating means to you personally. Ask yourself WHY you want to eat like that. Then declare that any thought, feeling, or impulse which suggests you won't do it between now and the day you die is Pig Squeal *(or Food Monster Noise, etc)* emanating from your reptilian brain. It's a biological error and you'll have nothing to do with it, so you'll ignore it from now on.

7. **"Don't wish it were easier, wish you were better" - Jim Rohn.** Look, it's going to take a little work to extinguish and replace the neurological pathways you've spent a lifetime reinforcing in your brain. You'll need to think through exactly how YOU want to eat, learn a few new ways of dis-empowering irrational food thoughts, and become a somewhat different person with food than you are now. That said, it's about the same amount of work that learning how to drive is. You need to take some time and study the rules of the road, practice a little bit *(ideally with some guidance and supervision)*... and then, you're free!
8. **Make your toughest food decisions in the morning.** Willpower is a fatigue-able muscle, kind of like gas in your tank. It's burned by decision making *(not just food decisions.)* There are only so many good decisions we can make each day. This is why so many people start out the day with the best of intentions but then fall apart in front of the fridge (or on the way home from work) in the evening. The fix? Make your decisions in the morning. Plan out what you're going to eat. Pack it all up in Tupperware if you need to. Have it waiting for you when you get home. Don't be stingy - make sure you'll feel well nourished. And for special bonus points, try to add an extra 2 x five minute decision-free-input-free breaks during the day to recharge. You'll be amazed how much easier nighttime eating control may become!
9. **Let me help you personally... click here to see how!**

The Science Behind Binge Eating

Two out of three adults living in the US are overweight! One out of three is obese! In just 70 years, the rates of obesity in men have risen from 10% to 33% and from 15% to 40% in women.

Does more than half the population lack the will power to avoid eating too much? Nonsense!

To understand the underlying reason, consider this experiment conducted by Milner and Olds over 50 years ago. These two researchers implanted electrodes in the pleasure centers of the brain in a group of rats, then connected those electrodes to a button the rats could press themselves to activate it.

The results were dramatic. The rats would press the lever thousands of times per hour to self-stimulate. They preferred self-stimulation to food and water, even when they were starving or dehydrated. Male rats would ignore a female in heat in order to keep self-stimulating. They would also cross shock-grids on the floor, enduring significant pain, to get to their lever. Female rats would abandon their nursing pups in order to press the lever.

A very cruel and interesting experiment *(which has been replicated several times in higher mammals).*

But what's even crueler is that Big Food companies may very well be using the exact same tactic on the US population. In today's America, food companies are primarily engineering food to activate their customer's pleasure centers.

Most chocolate bars contain 5 times more sugar than grapes.

Many commercial chips contain 12 times more salt than an onion of the same weight.

Is there any wonder we crave these foods? They are addictive BY DESIGN and the bottom line is simple: **You do NOT have a disease of the appetite! You are NOT broken. Overeating and binge eating are phenomena created by the big food companies.** They've changed the entire food supply system to create addicts out of massive parts of the population just to serve their bottom line, and every time you eat their food-like-substance there's probably some Fat Cat in a white suite with a mustache laughing all the way to the bank at your misery!

And it's not just Big Food.

The Big Advertising industry helps them convince you that you need their wares to survive.

And the Big Addiction Treatment industry tells you that you can't quit even if you wanted to ☹

Not convinced? Ask yourself if you believe there were any fat cavemen or cavewomen. Ask yourself if overeating was really a problem when we were evolving in the tropics with only fruit, vegetables, and perhaps some occasional wild animal protein *(depending upon what you believe about human nutrition – I personally think we're not meant to consume animals, but my book is diet agnostic.)*

Did Thag really look at Woola, grab his stomach and say "Woola, Thag eat too much grapes and leaves. Thag HIDEOUS. Look away Woola. Go make fire. Look away!"

I don't think so! Overeating is a modern problem created by modern industry.

To win this battle you must adopt a more powerful approach then simply listening to your body, because your body would love to eat Big Food's addictive products every time, which is why the Never Binge Again system relies on you thoroughly thinking through your own rules and aggressively separating your destructive thoughts about breaking these rules into a fictitious entity. That's how you can gain those extra microseconds at the moment of temptation to wake up, remember who you are, and make the right choice.

References:

➢ Milner, P. (1975). Models of Motivation and Reinforcement. In A. Wauquier & E. Rolls (Eds.), Brain-stimulation reward : a collection of papers prepared for the First International Conference on Brain-Stimulation Reward at Janssen Pharmaceutica, Beerse, Belgium on April 21-24: North-Holland Publishing Co.

Weight Loss – Never Binge Again Style

OK, so let's talk weight loss, Never Binge Again style! There are just three keys to success.

1. First, build and Follow Your OWN Custom Food Plan: Having a Food Plan doesn't mean you have to be hungry or stop eating all the foods you enjoy. It just means committing to a clear set of rules *(not guidelines!)* for your food intake which support your health, energy, fitness, and happiness goals.

Learning to follow your plan even when you're undergoing cravings, stress or emotional turmoil is
what the Never Binge Again system is really all about. If you haven't mastered this, please re-read the (free) Never Binge Again book, or investigate our unlimited coaching program to get personal help.

I typically recommend people forestall losing weight until after they've followed at least ONE food rules successfully for at least a few weeks. I want you to have the experience of SUCCESS and power over your Pig before you introduce anything else to the equation.

2. Create a mild-to-moderate workout regime which introduces a small caloric deficit: This is the second stumbling block a lot of people go through: They either don't exercise at all *(because they experience it with dread and hardship),* or they exercise so heavily as to exhaust and injure themselves. Maintaining a workout regime you can permanently enjoy and sustain is a wonderful enhancement for those who wish to drop the

pounds. *(LEGAL: Don't start exercising without permission from your doctor.)*

3. Understanding that IF you will genuinely Never Binge Again, losing weight is almost inevitable.

See, many, MANY people quit because they're not losing weight fast enough. What they don't understand, however, is that once you can design and follow a food plan, and exercise moderately, not only can you lose weight but you can keep it off forever! That's because if it's NOT working, you just make adjustments until it does, confident in your ability to STICK to those adjustments.

It's basic math and virtually inevitable. People who understand this become endlessly patient. They don't stress about their weight and they don't kill themselves with workouts in desperate attempts to make things happen fast. It's as if they've 'flipped a mental switch' and 6-12 months later they can just hit their goal with very little struggle.

Don't Become a Co-Conspirator in Your Own Oppression

The most dynamic professor I ever met was, without a doubt, Dr. Bruce Hare at S.U.N.Y Stony Brook. I still remember watching him get all worked up on the podium way back in 1984 *(when I still had hair and teeth!)*

It was SO inspiring, you felt like you were in church listening to a great minister, NOT taking a lecture at a university!

Dr. Hare passionately drove home the idea injustice could NOT take place unless the oppressed became co-conspirators in their own oppression:

- "Stop drinking the 'Kool Aid!'" he'd scream to the audience's cheers.

- "African Americans - stop using the N word!".

- "Minorities everywhere - stop making jokes about your own race!".

- "Stop consuming products which support corporate greed at the expense of the populace!".

All intoned in an emphatic, sing-song voice I can still hear echoing in my head to this day, but unfortunately, where Big Food is concerned, it seems people weren't listening. We are ALL, more or less, still co-conspiring with their lies, Allowing them to make literally TRILLIONS of dollars *($5.32 TRILLION in the US in 2015)* by cramming salt, sugar, fat, starch, and excitotoxic chemicals into a hyper-pleasurable-food-like-substance which they then package and advertise to APPEAR healthy.

To create and sell us "food drugs" which push our evolutionary pleasure buttons which tempt us to ignore self-care and normal, healthy nutrition.

That make us "high with food" at the expense of our health.

We gobble down their junk like a staving Doberman Pinscher scarfs down a rib roast.

Honestly, an apple doesn't stand a chance against the supercharged taste and stimulation engineered into a candy bar these days.

But if you're having trouble with those bars, or any other industrial food, you might consider how you've been made a co-conspirator in your own oppression.

That by willingly forking over your money to the big corporations for your daily poison.

That not only is that poison sapping your health and your mental energy.

But you're lining the pocked of MANY fat cat business people all too happy to dance on your early grave.

Thankfully, there IS a way out!

It starts with getting good n' mad about what's going on so you can stand up and say *(you might actually want to stand up and say this - it has an impact)*:

> I've had it with these companies profiting from MY misery. I'll be damned if I'm going to keep co-conspiring with their LEGAL equivalent of crack-cocaine for a mere 18 minutes of pleasure *(the average length of a sugar high).*
>
> At the expense of seriously burdening my body, my emotions, my productive work capacity, and my sense of well-being, all to keep me coming back for their tasty poison.
>
> I see now that my Inner Pig has made me a co-conspirator in my own oppression. And I simply won't take it anymore! Today I'll make just ONE Food Rule to protect myself from another industrial poison I KNOW I'm better off without or which I should seriously limit."

Don't sit and suffer for Big Food's benefit.

Get mad! Get healthy!

WANTED: Overeaters for Hazardous Battle with Demon Pig

WANTED: Overeaters for Hazardous Battle with Inner Demon Pig.

Initial Slow Results.

A few months of:

- Hunger bouts.
- Fending off attacks and cravings from Inner Binge Demon™.
- Fighting temptation at every turn.

But lifelong freedom from binge eating and food obsession upon success.

(All serious applicants accepted.)

Standing Up to Food Bullies

In our culture, we love and admire people who stand up to bullies -- especially when they defend others...whether these bullies are fictional movie bullies, like the Aryan-looking blonde guy on Karate kid who breaks Daniel-San's leg...or real live bullies like the people who tried to force Rosa Parks to sit on the back of the bus.

I'd like you to notice two very important things about bullies. The first is, in most cases, these bullies are quickly forgotten. They are the obstacle standing in the hero's path. They are just a detail in the story.

How many of you even remember the name of the blonde bully in The Karate Kid movie?

But more importantly, notice how you feel about people who stand up to a bully, even *(or perhaps especially)* if that bully keeps beating them down.

If you're anything like me, you feel an intense sense of comradery and admiration for ANYONE who stands up to a bully, no matter what the outcome.

Now...

I want you to adopt this approach to your Pig. See, your Pig IS a food Bully. And YOU are the one standing up to it! So, even if it knocks you down, even if you do overeat or binge.

Don't be too hard on yourself. Just stand up, dust yourself, and resume opposing the bully with 100% commitment and the totality of your being. **You should feel nothing but admiration and comradery for the part of yourself that opposes the bully – as you would for a real live hero.**

Because THAT is what you are...

A Hero!

And if you just keep standing up again you will win!

A Simple Tip to Deal with Food Pushers

Would you like a simple tip to deal with "food pushers" who want to know WHY you don't eat this or don't eat that? Try saying *"It's just not my thing"* and then just move on in the conversation.

Don't explain.

Don't educate.

Just say "It's just not my thing".

And that's all!

It works FAST on *most* food pushers so you can get back to your peaceful relationship with food.

Disputing Your Pig's Lies

Generally speaking, all you need to do is RECOGNIZE your Pig's Squeals so you can ignore them. However, sometimes they are very hard to recognize and/or extremely seductive. Many clients tell me their Pig is *extremely* stubborn too - it screams for junk, and no matter how many times they try to tell it to shut up and go back to its cage, it just becomes louder and louder, screaming and nagging until they cave in.

In these cases, with particularly stubborn, hard to hear, and/or seductive Pig Squeals, you may want to make an effort to logically dispute the arguments within them, at least one time. This moves the conversation from your lizard brain *(where the Pig reigns supreme)* to your Neocortex where logical thinking decimates the Demon's arguments and exposes the LIES they contain.

For example:

> PIG: It's midnight... I want some chocolate!
>
> YOU: No chance! Shut up and go to your cage!
>
> PIG: But I'm HUUUNGRRRRYYYYYY! You're going to starve. You worked out really hard today, you deserve it. We can afford some chocolate without gaining weight. It won't hurt at all!
>
> YOU: It's ok, I've eaten well throughout the day, I'm not going to starve, nobody is going to find my bones by the refrigerator, and the fact that I'm hungry just means I'm losing a bit of weight! Yippeee! Let it burn baby! Let it burn!
>
> PIG: But you had SUCH a rough day and you deserve to reward myself. Without chocolate life is miserable!!!!
>
> YOU: Silly Pig! Chocolate at midnight is not a reward, it's a punishment. I won't be able to sleep for hours, I'll wake up feeling bloated, fatter than before...and worst of all angry at myself for listening to your stupid ideas. The real reward is drinking a bit of water, going to sleep and waking up a little

thinner with a lot more confidence!

The benefit of exposing the lies in your Pig's argument is that its Squeals become infinitely easier to recognize and ignore. It's logic no longer holds sway with your higher mind, where all your most important goals reside.

Sometimes the Juice Ain't Worth the Squeeze

When you're making juice, there's inevitably a point of diminishing returns. I mean, you can get every last drop of juice out of the orange if you are extraordinarily determined, but the harder you work, the harder it is to get the next drop. You eventually get to a point where the extra juice you get just isn't worth the effort you've got to put in to get it. You're better off accepting a little waste and a less than perfect solution. Because you're either going to waste a LITTLE juice or a LOT of effort. Sometimes the juice ain't worth the squeeze.

I find it's similar with weight loss. Unless you're a competitive body builder, getting to your ideal weight requires more and more effort the closer you come to it. And when you're really close, you feel like you're fighting for every ounce.

For most overeaters, recovery means accepting a slightly less than perfect body. Letting go of the painful, self-critical voice you let your Pig develop inside your head to keep you feeling too weak to resist the next binge. At some point - which is a different weight for everyone - we all need to forgive ourselves for having a less than perfect body and it's VERY important to soften that self-critical voice no matter where you are on the journey towards your ideal weight too.

This is very different from thoroughly accepting our weight if it's unhealthy. It's more like we are accepting the fact that we are BECOMING a healthy person and loving ourselves for THAT. Maybe what that looks like is no longer focusing on having to lose 100 pounds, and shifting your attention instead to losing one pound, one hundred times. Regardless, sometimes the juice ain't worth the squeeze.

I wish someone told me this before I spend decades hating myself. Just because you don't NEED to love yourself more in order to stop overeating and binge eating doesn't mean you shouldn't love yourself more.

We could all do with a little more love in this life, I think.

Did You Kill Anyone on the Road Today?

I have a question for you.

Have you killed anyone on the road lately? Maybe you were driving in the scorching heat, and some idiot cut you off and nearly killed YOU so you got out of the car and bashed his head in with a club?

No? Are you sure? Don't be shy, I know some pretty good lawyers that might save you from the electric chair.

Ok, you didn't *(at least I hope you didn't because I'm not totally sure the attorneys will save you!)*

I get it, but did you ever WANT to kill someone on the road?

I'm guessing the answer is YES! Probably on numerous occasions.

Fortunately for you, when your reptilian brain reacted to the perceived attack by creating an urge to fight, your higher brain kicked in and said:

➢ "Hey, hey now, we can't really kill this guy. There's a law against murder. They'll throw us into a 4' by 4' prison cell with grey walls and a 300-pound cell mate named Bubba for life!"

Your higher brain overrode your Lizard brain's decision so you could abide by the rules defined by our society and preserve your well-being.

AND YOU CAN DO THE EXACT SAME THING WITH FOOD!

You can create a set of food rules that will become a part of who you are *("second nature")* forever so you don't have to constantly be vigilant and expend a lot of energy thinking about them every day.

These rules will override the food urges produced by the lizard brain (the Pig), be easy to remember and STILL allow you to eat delicious food you enjoy.

Plus, they'll reduce your urges to almost unperceived levels reasonably quickly.

It's a bit tricky to create rules that cover all of the above. You can do it yourself, or you can work with one of our very experienced coaches. Read the details and grab your spot below while we're still offering this:

www.NeverBingeAgainCoaching.com

Those Who Believe Absurdities Can Commit Atrocities

"Those Who Can Make You Believe Absurdities Can Make You Commit Atrocities" - Voltaire

The food industry wants you to believe much of their industrially processed food is healthy, that you can get all the nutrition you need from a cardboard box, a bar full of chemicals with fancy wrapping paper on it, or a black hole of sugar, starch, salt, and oil backed by millions in advertising.

Your Pig wants you to believe taking one bite, taste, or swallow off of your carefully constructed Food Plan won't hurt.

Or that you've been good long enough to justify a Binge.

Or that you're healthy enough to tolerate it.

Or that other people will abandon you if you eat healthy.

Or that you'll be "too deprived" if you abstain from Pig Slop.

Or that you've tried and failed so many times before there's simply no point in trying again.

And the addiction treatment industry wants you to believe you've got a chronic, progressive, mysterious disease.

That you're powerless over the impulse to overeat.

That you can't QUIT harming yourself with food.

That the best you can do is abstain one day at a time.

And only if you hang out with other people who believe this nonsense.

And make yourself entirely dependent on other people who haven't solved the problem themselves.

With all these absurdities so readily accepted by our culture, how can ANYONE be expected to eat healthy?

Question authority! Reject the insanity!

You have FULL control over your legs, hands, lips, mouth, and tongue. You have a brain in your head, and you can figure out what's healthy vs. what's Pig Slop.

Question authority, reject the insanity, and eat healthy.

It's Literally Impossible to Fail

I talk to a lot of people who say they've TRIED Never Binge Again with SOME success but they really don't think it can "Work" for them in the long run and they want to try "something else."

I'm always a little puzzled by this very strange idea. You see, Never Binge Again is NOT like a gastric bypass, a pharmaceutical pill, or a therapeutic "treatment." It's NOT something I do TO you or FOR you to MAKE you stop Binging. It's just the systematic application of common sense, free will, and responsibility in a ruthless manner:

- ➢ We systematically and ruthlessly identify all your trigger foods and eating behaviors
- ➢ Then we clarify the healthiest decisions you can possibly make when confronted by them
- ➢ We commit to those decisions as a matter of character
    - ✓ The kind of person you are
    - ✓ Or the kind of person you are becoming
- ➢ And then we define any thought or feeling which suggests we will ever act in the most remote way otherwise as our destructive self
    - ✓ Or our Pig
    - ✓ Our fat thinking self
    - ✓ Etc.

This simple set of common-sense techniques then clarifies our thinking enough that we can purge our minds of doubt and uncertainty so we can concentrate 100% of our effort on the goal. If we happen to make a mistake we just get up and refocus our minds once again with 100% effort, just like an Olympic Archer re-focuses on the bulls-eye with crystal clear vision at every pull of the arrow.

The ONLY way to fail at Never Binge Again is to either reject common sense or consciously choose to let the Pig out of its Cage. And so I always ask people who say "It's not working", WHAT IS THE ALTERNATIVE?

- ➢ Would it be better to shoot for a fuzzy goal? To play "blind archery" and NOT define what healthy eating is for yourself? I don't think so! My grandfather always said "if you don't know where you're going you'll probably wind up someplace else!"

- ➢ Should we avoid clarifying what a healthy food thought is vs. a destructive one? I can't see how that does anyone any good. You've got to recognize the healthy ones to act on them and the unhealthy ones to avoid them, right?

- ➢ Should we just "try to eat healthy" and do the best we can? Well, if that worked for you I don't think you'd be reading this!

- ➢ Should we seek out some new diet guru for the forty-seven-millionth time? Well, read their books if you want to but in the end you STILL must embrace their very specific set of Food Rules and learn how to catch yourself trying to talk yourself out of following it.

- ➢ Should we disclaim all responsibility and power over our ability to control ourselves and pretend we have some mysterious, chronic, progressive disease, then spend our lives confessing our troubles in the town square with other

> helpless people who have this fake disease too? Should we spend nights away from our families talking about how we just can't control ourselves and need to cultivate fear of our own healthy appetites? That would be a VERY dismal view of humanity, don't you think? To say "we can't control ourselves with food" is really to say we are nothing more than animals and I think human beings are MUCH more than that, don't you?

I SAY NO THANK YOU!!!! But I understand why people are afraid to be disappointed. I feel their pain because I previously tried a thousand times and failed. But if you adopt the attitude of playing the 'never binge again' game and resolve to be 100% committed to your food plan and caging the pig but are forgiving to yourself and resume the 'never binge again' game if you make a mistake. Then there is literally NO way to 'fail', you can only STUMBLE and if you keep getting up the 'never binge again' way of life virtually MUST take over your thinking completely so you can truly think like a permanently thin person.

Am I right or am I right?

Food for thought!

My Two Favorite Quotes of All Time

"You Can Have Anything You Want But You Can't Have Everything You Want" – Peter McWilliams

"A Life of Discipline is Better Than a Life of Regret" – Jim Rohn

Really, you can eat anything you want to if you're willing to pay the consequences. You can eat a box of donuts one day per month if you're steady and reliable with your nutrition the rest of the time. You probably won't want to because it feels too good to eat well and you won't want to sacrifice that to spend the next 72 hours recovering from donuts, but the point is you

COULD if that was the life you so choose.

Similarly, you can have a bodybuilder's physique if you're willing to work out several hours per day, eat scrupulously well, and sacrifice enough on other fronts. You might not choose to make this trade off, but you could if you wanted to, no matter how badly you've treated yourself in the past (within limits).

Probably you'll choose something not quite so extreme.

But you can have anything you want with enough focus, dedication, and discipline.

Discipline is what gives you the freedom to become anything you want to become.

So, choose a rule and get started. Nobody's going to boss you around, but nobody's going to do it for you either.

I've never regretted installing a new discipline in my life. Flossing my teeth. Not eating chocolate. Exercising 6 days per week. Writing at least ten minutes a day.

I've regretted the disciplines I put off or never did.

And on my death bed I'm pretty sure I'm not going to say "Geez, I wish I never bothered flossing, writing, or exercising". I'm pretty sure I'm going to be grateful for the time and energy I put into those things.

While There is Breath in Your Body

While there is breath in your body there is the opportunity for a new and different life.

Your Inner Pig may suggest it is too late:

- Too late to eat better

- Too late to exercise
- Too late to be a better mother, father, sister, brother, spouse, employee, or friend
- Too late to think positively
- Too late to break free from depression and anxiety
- Too late to earn money
- Too late to find love
- Too late to enjoy your life

But having talked intimately with more than 1,000 people and having come through my own personal crisis, I can tell you beyond a shadow of a doubt it is not!

You can remake yourself at any moment and live out the balance of your life in ways you never dreamed possible.

All you need to do is use the present moment to turn the wheel and get OFF the binge eating highway and ON a path to where you most desire.

No matter how difficult, no matter how much "you can't", "you won't", "you've tried 1,000 times before", "you're hopeless", "you're pathetic", "don't even bother", "circumstances don't permit", etc. you may hear coming from that crazy little head of yours.

YOU CAN AND YOU WILL!
(But only if you say you will)

Will you?

Why I Really Hate Your Pig!

Being obese and/or overweight as a result of binge eating doesn't just effect your health and energy level. I think the WORST thing about it is how it effects your state of mind. Clients have told me things like:

"My friends call me "Fatty" and "Fat-Bastard" as a joke - but it's killing me"

"I am not on social media because I'm ashamed of how I look"

"I don't know if I'll ever be loved"

"Doctors tell me that I can't get pregnant because I'm too fat"

"I don't go to amusement parks or the theater because the seats are too small and I won't fit"

"I dread the idea of going shopping for clothes - It's so embarrassing"

"Parties and social events should be a fun time - but I absolutely hate them! I hate how I look, I hate that people will think I'm fat so I avoid parties altogether"

That is why I HATE YOUR PIG *(even though I love you!)*. It's destroying your self-worth. It's isolating you from your friends and family. It's robbing you of love and fun and intimacy (every type) just so it can binge on its Slop.

Well, I say the heck with that!!! You deserve to walk the earth as a confident, healthy person, and more importantly, to be loved and desired! So let's begin the journey out of the prison your Pig put you in OK?

One Last Critical Thing Before You Go!

There's one more thing before you go and it's really, REALLY important.

Something I've been meaning to tell you all book long...

And that thing is...

I LOVE YOU.

I love you for even CONSIDERING integrating Never Binge Again into your life.

I love you for not letting your Inner Pig put down my book in a fit of rage to never let you look at it again..

I love you for making even ONE Food Rule.

And even TRYING to implement it.

I love you for entertaining the idea that our culture is entirely wrongheaded about food.

That you are not so much sick and diseased as you are victimized by an industry which has targeted your lizard brain using sophisticated food processing, persuasion, and advertising methods.

I love you for choosing to get up, time and again if necessary, after your Pig has knocked you down.

After you've felt alone, ashamed, and desperate to fix your food problem.

After your Pig had you convinced there was truly no hope.

I love you for wanting to be present for your children and your grandchildren.

To be the role model your mother or father couldn't be for you even though your Pig would MUCH rather you sat on the couch watching TV with a great big feed bag over your mouth looking for love at the bottom of a bag, box, or container Where there is NO love! *(I promise you there's NOT, I looked hard for thirty years - if it were there, I would've found it by now!)*

After having lived an exceptionally difficult and painful life filled with binge eating for more than thirty years and unfortunately finding out very late in life the incredible power to STOP I've unknowingly had at my disposal all this time.

And in case your journey has been similar to mine *(God forbid)...*

I just want you to know this...

In case you never hear it from anybody else...

I BELIEVE IN YOU.

(You) can do it.

You CAN stop binge eating, overeating, and constantly criticizing yourself.

If there is breath in your body, you absolutely CAN.

Hang in there. It will get better if you let it.

It WILL.

I can't say it enough... I believe in you. And I'd like to help.

Peace Out!

APPENDIX: FRANKLY I'M PUZZLED

Frankly, I'm puzzled. It's difficult for me to totally understand what's going on.

See, I run into so many people who say Never Binge Again makes PERFECT sense to them, but they're putting off doing something about it.

- **Some of them are frightened of using the words Never and Always.** but I explain to them we only use these in the same way we'd tell a two-year-old little girl that she could NEVER cross the street without holding our hand. It's just too dangerous for her to even consider. Even though we know when she gets older, we'll teach her to look both ways on her own.

  Similarly, we present our Food Rules to our Food Demon as if they were set in stone, even though we know we can change them later. (That lets us purge our minds of doubt and distraction and focus all our energy on the goal).

- **Some people are afraid of feeling too guilty if they make a mistake.** "I'll just beat myself up and that'll make it worse." Well, perseverating on guilt DOES make things worse because it makes you feel too weak to resist the next binge.

That's why we recommend you only feel guilty long enough to pay attention to what happened, make any adjustments necessary to your food rules, and make a go-forward plan. You DO want to feel uncomfortable briefly, just like you want to feel pain if you touch a hot stove, so you don't do it again but getting overly involved with the guilt is definitely NOT encouraged!

- **Some are afraid we'll force them to give up some food treat they don't want to give up.** But NOBODY is going to tell you what to eat! Dependency is actually a central part of addiction and we actively discourage it. We just help people come up with and stick to their OWN Food Rules.
- **Some people are afraid Never Binge Again works for other people but just can't work for them.** First of all, that's their Food Demon talking - a perfect excuse to keep overeating. But even if things "don't work" for you, our program is 100% guaranteed. If you don't feel it dramatically changes your relationship with food (entirely based on YOUR opinion) you get every dime back. I don't want your money if I can't actually help you! See the site below for details.

So why not fix this food problem once and for all? You've literally got nothing to lose but your belly...and there's no reason not to start yesterday! Click below for more info now:

www.NeverBingeAgainCoaching.com

Made in the USA
Middletown, DE
21 September 2019